PUFF

Lemmings Adv
THE GEN

Lemmings

Adventure Gamebook 1

The Genesis Quest

**Nigel Gross and
Jon Sutherland**

PUFFIN BOOKS

PUFFIN BOOKS

Published by the Penguin Group
Penguin Books Ltd, 27 Wrights Lane, London W8 5TZ, England
Penguin Books USA Inc., 375 Hudson Street, New York, New York 10014 USA
Penguin Books Australia Ltd, Ringwood, Victoria, Australia
Penguin Books Canada Ltd, 10 Alcorn Avenue, Toronto, Ontario, Canada M4V 3B2
Penguin Books (NZ) Ltd, 182–190 Wairau Road, Auckland 10, New Zealand

Penguin Books Ltd, Registered Offices: Harmondsworth, Middlesex, England

First published in Puffin Books 1995
3 5 7 9 10 8 6 4 2

Lemmings copyright © Psygnosis Ltd, 1995
Text copyright © Nigel Gross and Jon Sutherland, 1995
Illustrations copyright © Selecciones Ilustradas, 1995
All rights reserved

The moral right of the authors has been asserted

Typeset by Datix International Limited, Bungay, Suffolk
Filmset in Monophoto Palatino
Made and printed in Great Britain by Clays Ltd, St Ives plc

Except in the United States of America, this book is sold subject
to the condition that it shall not, by way of trade or otherwise, be lent,
re-sold, hired out, or otherwise circulated without the publisher's
prior consent in any form of binding or cover other than that in
which it is published and without a similar condition including this
condition being imposed on the subsequent purchaser

THE WORLD ACCORDING TO THE LEMMINGS

The Lemmings, as perhaps you already know, live on the ISLAND. This is a special place and one for which the Lemmings — although they don't know it — are perfectly suited.

The Island is a place full of puzzles and traps to catch an unwary Lemming, and the Lemmings love it. As least they would if they ever stopped to think about it. You see, that involves the two things the Lemmings never really did: Stopping and Thinking! Lemmings like to move, they like to dance, they like to jump, they like to dig, in fact they like to DO most things and do those things in lots of different ways.

Over the years the Lemmings have formed into 12 different tribes, each doing lots of things in their own way. There are the medieval Lemmings, who just love to party in old-fashioned clothes; then there's the Classical Lemmings: they're very traditional and love digging. Highland Lemmings like music, and Shadow Lemmings like the dark, so many opportunities to bump into things!

They all live together on the Island but keep to their own parts. No one can say how long this has been going on as Lemmings don't worry very much about time — well, not unless it involves getting stuck into something, or getting out of something, or digging through something, or falling over something.

Anyway, all of this is what the Lemmings do, and usually that's about it. Unfortunately, every once in a while the Lemmings get an urge. It starts off as just a vague feeling, then it grows and grows till they just can't resist it. They simply must do it. But what? Well, it's like this: Lemmings don't take much interest in history and such like, but deep in every Lemming's memory is a picture of when all the Lemmings lived together and were, well, more or less the same. Now the Lemmings don't really want to be all the same again, but there's an old legend that says ... well it goes a bit like this: 'Old days ... a Medal, we all got a bit, now we got to bring it together.'

Not a lot of it really, is there? But, then again, what would you expect from Lemmings!

Translated into English, this means that each tribe of Lemmings must find its piece of the Great Medallion so that it can be put back together again. There's not much in the legend about what happens if the Lemmings fail, but it's probably pretty bad!

Now all this may sound OK, but getting all the parts of the medallion is not as easy as it sounds; after all, Lemmings are prone to the odd accident or two! By themselves, the Lemmings are going to find this a little tricky – a plan needs to be thought out ... not a strong point of the Lemmings.

Now this is where YOU come in. The Lemmings are ready and willing, and all they need is a bit of direction and perhaps a little luck, and the Great Lemming Quest is GO!

INTRODUCTION

This is a gamebook. You may have read lots of them before — but just in case you haven't, we thought we'd better tell you: you don't read this book like you would a normal book, starting at the first page and ending with the last. In *The Genesis Quest* YOU decide how the Lemmings will find all the separate parts of the Great Medallion. The Lemmings are good at lots of things, but thinking isn't one of them. You're going to have to do that for them. If you make the right choices, then the Lemmings will succeed, but if you make the wrong ones, well, you'll soon find out!

Playing the Game

In *The Genesis Quest* you will guide the Lemmings through many tricks, traps and puzzles.

This book is divided into 400 paragraphs, each with a number: the first one is **1** and the last one is **400** — but you don't read through them in number order. Instead, each paragraph ends with a number of choices. By the side of each of these choices, a number is printed in **bold** type. Once you have decided what you want the Lemmings to do, find the paragraph with that number, then continue reading. Keep on doing this until you have either finished the adventure or failed along the way.

Unlike a lot of gamebooks, there isn't a lot of fighting in this one. Lemmings can fight if they really have to, but violence doesn't really appeal. If the Lemmings do get into a sticky position, then you'll be told how to fight in the main text.

To start off playing *The Genesis Quest*, all you need is a pencil, a piece of scrap paper and a normal six-sided dice.

In this book you get to control eight tribes of Lemmings. Each tribe has its own special abilities and its own special problems. You decide in which order to play the zones; if you get stuck in one zone, you can leave and go on to another — but be warned, you will have to finish all eight zones to complete the quest.

To start off with, you get 50 Lemmings. There's lots of dangers along the way, so although 50 may sound like a lot, you're going to have to be very careful with them! At the end of each zone you will be given five more Lemmings to play with as a reward. The type of Lemmings you can have depends on the zone you're in (the book will tell you when you need to make this choice and also what types you can have).

Because there are so many different types, here's a list that may help you make the right choices later on:

Jumper	Filler	Runner	Ballooner
Archer	Attractor	Bomber	Scooper
Hopper	Skater	Kayaker	Swimmer
Roller	Thrower	Digger	Club Basher
Shimmier	Climber	Builder	Basher
Miner	Floater	Exploder	Laser Blaster
Magno Boots	Bazooka	Spearer	Fencer
Stomper	Skier	Mortar	Pole Vaulter
Platformer	Diver	Super Lem!	Flame Thrower
Surfer	Parachute	Slider	Jet Pack
Roper	Twister	Glue Pourer	Icarus Wings
Musician	Blocker	Sledger	

Most of the names are self-explanatory and you'll soon find out what the others do as you start to read the book.

Now it's time to go to **1**, where you can decide which zone you'd like to play first.

The Party

Things Collected

Medallion

Notes

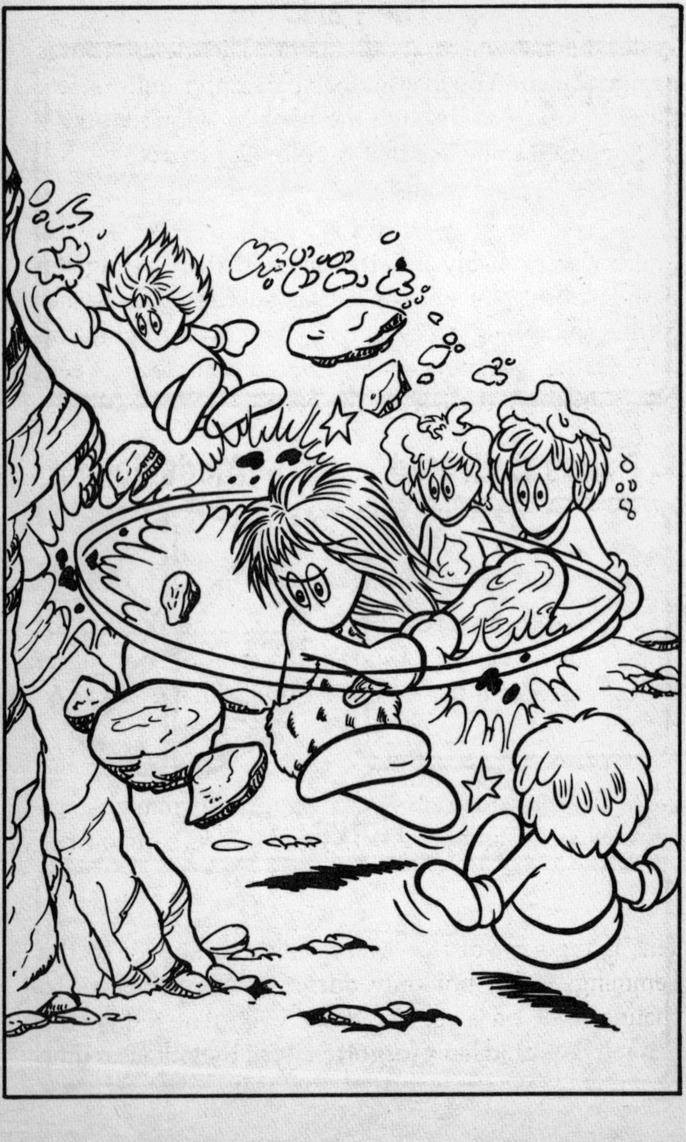

1

Well, this is where it all starts. The next stop is paragraph **20**. You'll visit that paragraph quite a few times as you read through the book . . . Don't worry — it's supposed to be like that . . . Now go to **20**.

2

There was probably a better method than letting the Basher loose! Not known for his subtlety, the Basher carries on bashing everything in sight. In the confusion two of the Lemmings are knocked senseless: 'Yeee-oww!!' (remove them from the party).

The others meanwhile are covered from head to foot in rock dust. What fun! Go to **345**.

3

Roll one dice and add the result to the number of Ropers in the party. If this gives a total of 9 or more, then go to **180**. If the total is 8 or less, then go to **216**.

4

Now the rubble is out of the way, the Lemmings can either carry straight on (go to **259**) or turn left (go to **214**).

5

This is the start of the 'Maze'. It's well known to the Lemmings — but not only does the Maze manage to change itself on a regular basis; even if it didn't, the Lemmings would have forgotten what they did last time anyway!

6

To make matters worse, the whole place is practically in total darkness. The local Lemmings are used to this, but it may make things a little tricky for you.

There are three paths for you to take from here. One goes a little bit to the left (go to **84**); one is a middling sort of path (go to **57**); and the third wanders off to the right (go to **99**).

6

Just in time, the Builders manage to construct a bridge across the pool, and the Lemmings make it safely to the platform.

Go to **81**.

7

The Lemmings have reached the edge of the ice field. To the east, the icy-cold polar seas stretch to the horizon.

Which way will the Lemmings go now: west (go to **184**) or will they go south, along the coast (go to **78**)?

8

There's just no shifting the Skaters off the ice. Eventually one or two get tired and rejoin the party, but you still have to leave the last two behind. Remove them from the party, and then head towards the snowfield.

Go to **156**.

9

Thinking about it, this was bound to happen, wasn't it? You can't blame the Lemmings for this, they're not supposed to think! YOU ARE!!!

Go back to **385** and try something different. You may also, if you wish, write 'FOOL' on your forehead in felt-tip pen – only, judging by your past performance, you'll probably do it looking in the mirror and write 'LOOF' instead!

10

The Diggers dig, the crabs nip. 'Yeow!' shout the Diggers.

The tide is coming in and the Lemmings have to give up. Oh well, that's the way it goes – sometimes...

Your adventure ends here

11

... a Flame-throwing Thing. A huge, rusty boiler blocks the entire platform and belches out great plumes of flame and steam. The whole thing is balanced on a pillar, several metres off the ground.

Take it from us, there's no way the Lemmings are going to get over this obstacle, so what are they going to do?

Going through or under the pillar looks possible. Which type of Lemming will you choose: a Basher (go to **135**), a Miner (go to **73**), an Exploder (go to **25**) or a Blocker (go to **101**)?

12

Gradually, this path winds its way into the forest. It seems to be going slowly downhill. Here and there stagnant pools of water lie on the ground.

Trying hard to avoid them, go to **16**.

13

The water is running very fast, and it is so cold that the Lemmings soon start to go numb. They are almost across when disaster strikes! Three Lemmings lose their grip and are washed away in the current, never to be seen again!

You may choose which Lemmings have been washed away. Remove them from the list of party members, then go to **255**.

14

Things are going very well. But which way will the diggers go now? Shall they carry on the same way (go to **122**) or turn sharply to the left (go to **356**)?

15

Well, with your help the Lemmings have succeeded in bringing back all the parts of the Medallion. It's time for the Lemmings to have a serious party now and see if anyone can remember what happens next!

And that's about the end of the Great Lemming Quest.

Oh yes, just one more thing: go to **400**.

16

The Lemmings find themselves standing on the edge of a murky-looking pond. There is the buzz of mosquitoes and the odd plopping sound as a fish breaks the surface.

'Yeow!' a Lemming yells out from somewhere near the back.

Then another lets out a shout as the mosquitoes home in.

Perhaps it would be wise to move on. They can walk round the pond (go to **319**). Or they can turn southwest (go to **139**).

17

The Musician pulls out his lute (that's an old-fashioned guitar-shaped sort of thing to you and me) and starts to play . . . awfully! What a racket!

In three seconds flat, the Dragon can stand it no longer and is out of the cavern with both front paws clasped firmly over its ears!

Nice one, Lemmings. Now go to **306**.

18

Roll one dice and add the number rolled to the number of Builders in the party.

If the total is 8 or more, then go to **6**. If the total is 7 or less, then go to **35**.

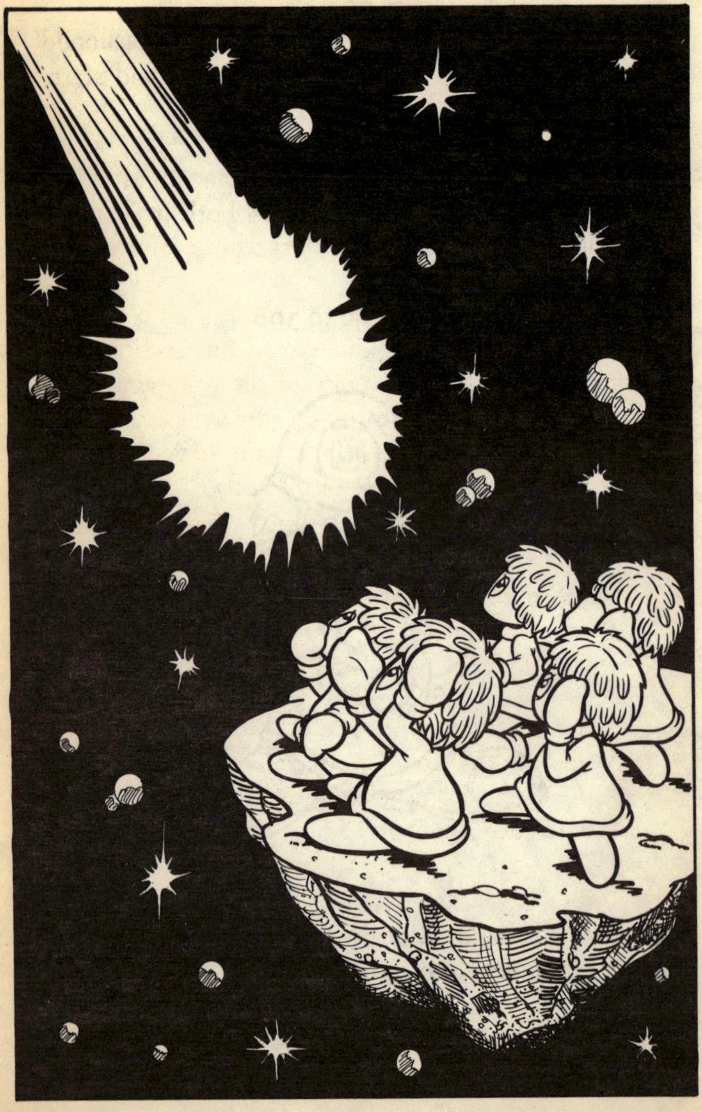

19
The comet speeds through the Space Zone. This is the way to travel!

Or is it? Go to **53**.

20
This is the place where you make those choices that really count!

If this is the first time you have read this section, then you may choose from any one of the following eight zones. As you progress through, you will (hopefully!) complete some of them. Once you have beaten a zone, be sure to make a note of the fact.

If you have successfully completed a zone, you may add five extra Lemmings to your party's strength.

From here you may:

- play the Medieval Zone, go to **336**.
- play the Shadow Zone, go to **22**.
- play the Circus Zone, go to **376**.
- play the Space Zone, go to **395**.
  play the Sports Zone, go to **173**.
  play the Classic Zone, go to **320**.
  play the Polar Zone, go to **118**.
  play the Beach Zone, go to **43**.

If you have successfully completed all eight zones without cheating, then please go to **15**.

21

The spaceship judders violently and then starts to move.

Hmm, that must have been the 'ON' switch.

Roll one dice. If the result is 3 or more, then go to **129**. If the result is 2 or less, then go to **79**.

22

Welcome to the Shadow Zone. This is a rather odd part of the Lemming island – which is really saying something when you think what the rest of it is like! This place is permanently in darkness, it's sinister and really rather scary. Still, the local Lemmings love it . . .

This is the start of the Shadow Zone. Before you go any further, you must select the Lemmings that will go on this part of the quest. How many you can have depends on the number of Lemmings you finished the last zone with. Simply trade in the Lemmings you already have for the new ones listed below on a one-for-one basis. If this is the first zone you have visited, then you may choose 50 Lemmings.

Lemmings available in the Shadow Zone

Flame Thrower	Parachute	Attractor
Hopper	Climber	Shimmier
Glue Pourer	Fencer	Archer

Once you have done this, make a note of the ones you have chosen, then go to **94**.

23

Hmm, here comes a simple (did we say simple!) T-junction. It's a case of go left (go to **201**) or right (go to **260**).

24

Roll one dice and add the result to the number of Pole Vaulters in the party; then make a note of this number.

Now go to **253**.

25

Not a bad idea, really. Unfortunately the Exploders don't stand still while they're waiting to explode, and this one starts pacing backwards and forwards ...

Go to **124**.

26

Oh yes, this is more like it ... a choice of one! Go to **302**.

27

The Flame Thrower lets rip with a blast of fire, and the rubble disintegrates.

Congratulations! The Shadow Lemmings have succeeded in spite of you ... oh, sorry ... with your help!

Make a note of this, and then go to **20**.

28

'If in doubt, just move around aimlessly', goes the old Lemming proverb, and that's just what the Space Lemmings do. So, go to **204**.

29

The Blocker turns into an Exploder. Since it is already a Blocker, it stands stock still at the base of the pillar!

Go to **190**.

30

At last the Lemmings are getting their sight back as the effect of the dazzling light wears off. Somehow they have managed to find their way along a passage with three bottomless pits in it! Now go to **128**.

31

Suddenly there's no floor! Before the Lemmings know what's happened, three of them have fallen into an unseen pit. Remove three Lemmings of your choice from the party, and then go to **348**.

32

Well, here we are, and there's the Medallion!

Make a note of your success, and then go to **20**.

WELL DONE!

33

The moment of truth has arrived and the overall champions of the Games are going to be announced. If they win, the Sports Lemmings will get their piece of the Medallion; if they lose ... well, that doesn't bear thinking about!

Go to **311**.

34

Now the Lemmings are across the rock pool, it's only a short walk to 'X marks the spot', which appears to be a large sandcastle. The Medallion — so the Lemmings reckon — is hidden in the middle of this castle.

Hmm, the first thing that needs to be done is to get through the castle's walls. Now where are those Diggers? You'd better have some with you, 'cos there's no way through without them.

If there are Diggers in the party, then go to **85**.

If there aren't any Diggers left in the party then it's ... wait for it ...

Your adventure ends here!

35

The Builders work as fast as they can, but they just fail to make it in time, and two Lemmings tumble into the pool. Remove two Lemmings of your choice from the party, and then go to **81**.

36

After a surprisingly long walk, the Lemmings come to a complex junction. The Lemmings are having a whale of a time, all of them totally confused and lost, and they are *loving it!* They (and you) can now turn sharp right (go to **178**), turn hard left (go to **143**), turn slightly left (go to **23**), or turn slightly right (go to **201**).

37

The barrel, which is rather large, seems to have some kind of tap on the side of it.

Do you want the Lemmings to walk really close to the barrel (go to **137**)? Or will they retreat and go down the stairs (go to **342**)?

38

Somehow the Lemmings manage to tear themselves away from the clowns, but it wasn't easy and there are more than a few moans and groans. However, at least now the Lemmings have reached the far side of the ring, go to **281**.

39

Finally the word goes out: the judges have reached a decision!

Go to **382**.

40

The floor of the forest is littered with dried leaves that give a loud crack whenever a Lemming stands on one. It seems as if they've been in the forest for ever. Without the sun, it's difficult to tell whether it's still daytime.

The track slowly starts to curve around to the right. Following the path, go to **108**.

41

The Glue Pourer produces a large pot and tips out some glue. This is pretty useful stuff, this glue, and in no time a firm but rather sticky bridge of glue stretches across to the far platform.

Go to **32**.

42

The Circus Lemmings start their quest just outside the BIG TOP. This is the biggest circus tent in the whole zone, and also the most dangerous!

Inside the Big Top lurk all kinds of dangers for an unwary Lemming, and unfortunately there's no way of getting this part of the Medallion without spending quite some time inside . . . so go to **132**.

43

Welcome to the Beach Club. This is the home of the Beach Lemmings and their chief, the rather well-known Barbaranne Lemming.

This is one of the coolest places on the island. The Lemmings are so laid back it's a wonder they don't just fall over!

This is the start of the Beach Zone. Before you go any further, you must select the Lemmings that will go on this part of the quest. How many you have depends on the number of Lemmings you finished the last zone with. Simply trade in the Lemmings you already have for the new ones listed below on a one-for-one basis. If this is the first zone you have visited, then you may choose 50 Lemmings.

Lemmings available in the Beach Zone

Jumper	Surfer	Ballooner
Attractor	Shimmier	Builder
Digger	Diver	Runner

Once you have done this, make a note of the ones you have chosen, and then go to **119**.

44

This is the pentathlon, the final event in the games. There are five separate stages to this event and the 110-metre hurdles is the first.

Now, although the pentathlon has five stages in it, it is still a single event, and a Lemming may be used only once. Therefore, if you use all your Runners in this stage, then you may not use them in the next one!

As well as this, the Lemmings can't remember what other events in the pentathlon are going to be!

So which Lemmings are going to run in the hurdles? You can pick as many or as few as you like. Make a note of your choice, and then go to 374.

45

You are in a huge expanse of rough ground, hemmed in on all sides by iron walls. The Lemmings could always go back the way they've just come. No, not really!

This looks like a job for a Miner. If you haven't got any then . . .

Your adventure ends here

If you have got some, then go to 275.

46

The platform continues for a short distance before its path is blocked by . . . Go to 11.

47

To get a Gold Medal, the Lemmings need to have scored 12 points; to get a Silver, 10 points; and a Bronze, 8 points.

Make a note of any medals the Lemmings may have won, and then it's time for the next round of events; go to 237.

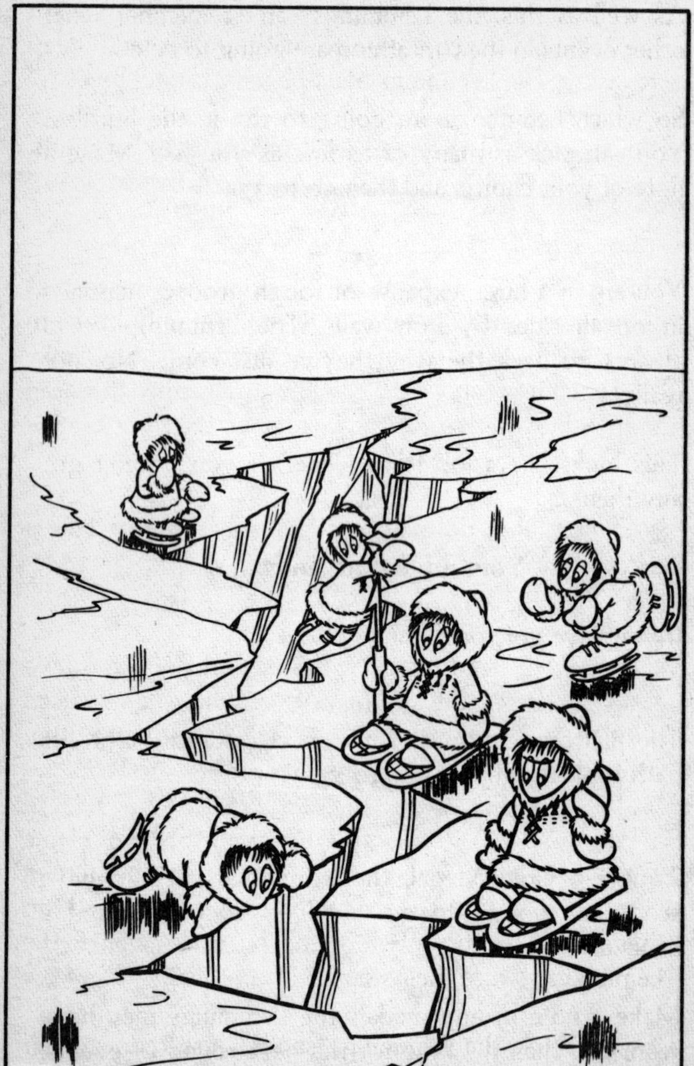

48

The ice field is criss-crossed with gullies and deep crevasses. The Lemmings must be very careful here!

Which way will they go: west (go to **246**) or southwest (go to **196**)?

49

This is another straightforward event: run as fast as you can and jump as far as you can, the only problem being not to step over the line. Obviously the closer the Lemmings can get to the line, the further they can jump — but the bigger the chance of stepping on the line and getting disqualified.

What will they do: play it safe (go to **183**) or take a chance (go to **227**)?

50

A Flame Thrower will be able to get rid of the rubble easily. Unfortunately, each Flame Thrower can be used only once. If the Flame Thrower is used, you may remove the rubble and then go to **4**.

If you decide to do this, make a note that one Flame Thrower is now 'out of fuel'. You'd best be careful here since, as we have already told you, there's no guarantee that the rubble won't be back again if the Lemmings retrace their steps!

If you think the Lemmings should just retrace their steps and try another path, then go to **93**.

51

Without a Flame Thrower, the Shadow Lemmings have had it.

Your adventure ends here ... so close and yet so far ...

52

Ah, looks as if this is going to be the high jump ...

Go to 339.

53

The comet, with the Lemmings aboard, is heading straight for an asteroid field.

Oops! What now? Should they jump off (go to 144) or stay put and hope (go to 28)?

54

The Lemmings are now standing on another platform. There is a flight of stairs leading down, (go to 342).

Alternatively, there is a large barrel over to the left. If you want the Lemmings to go and have a look at the barrel, then go to 37.

55

The Stomper immediately starts jumping up and down in the way that only a Stomper can. A hole soon appears and the Lemmings dive through it.

Go to 288.

56

Lots more ice here! The Lemmings seem to have been wandering around in the ice field for ages. Perhaps you'd better think about getting them out fairly soon.

Which way now: south (go to **384**) or west (go to **111**)?

57

Very soon, the Lemmings come to a three-way junction in the path. Here, you can go leftish (go to **178**), bear right (go to **249**) or walk down the middle (go to **201**).

58

There's no time to bandy words with the Troll. If he won't get out of the way by himself, then the Lemmings must make him get out of the way!

The Troll raises the club and swings it towards the nearest Lem . . .

The Lemmings are going to fight the Troll.

The Troll has a FIGHTING SCORE of 10.

Work out the Lemmings' score by adding 1 for each Archer in the party and ½ for each Basher and Thrower (remembering that an odd ½ does not count).

Once you have done this, roll one dice and add the result to the troll's score, then do the same for the Lemmings' score.

If the Lemmings have scored the same as or more than the Troll, then go to **75**. If the Troll has scored more, then go to **98**.

59

Just the job! The Filler moves to the edge of the hole, and in no time the hole's been filled.

Now go to **284**.

60

Roll one dice and add the result to the number of Diggers in the party.

If this totals 9 or more, then go to **141**. If the result is 8 or less, then go to **10**.

61

Suddenly there's no more maze ...

'YIPPEE!!!'

Congratulations, you have guided the Lemmings safely out of one of the hardest mazes ever!

From here there's just a wide flat platform ... Go to **383**.

62

BOOM ... the Lemming flies through the air in a graceful arc ...

'YIPPEE!'

Unfortunately, the Lemming begins to fall, far short of the platform, and crashes back to the ground with a thump. Remove this badly bruised Lemming from the party (you choose which type).

Now go back to **267** and have another go.

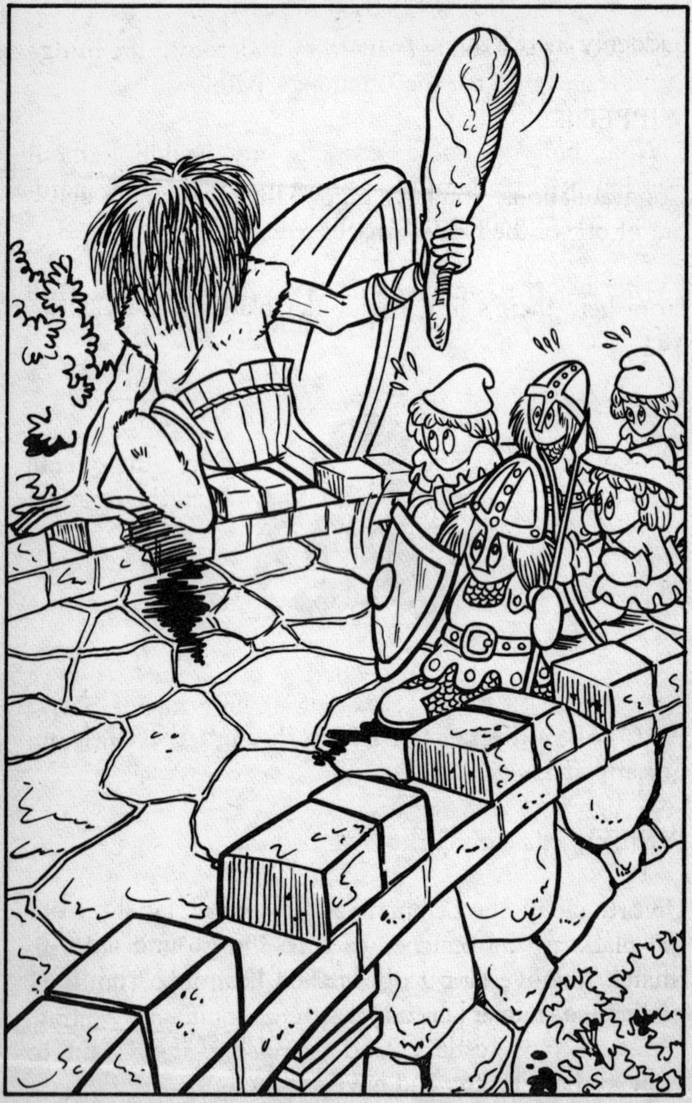

63

Suddenly the Troll appears from underneath the bridge and leaps up to bar the Lemmings' path.

'What be you doing, crossing my bridge without asking first?' it demands, baring its teeth at the Herdman, and tapping a huge wooden club against its leg.

What will the Lemmings do? Will they fight the Troll (go to **58**)? Or should they speak to the Troll (go to **131**)?

64

Congratulations! The Sports Lemmings are the overall champions of the Games and are awarded their part of the Medallion as a prize.

Make a note of this fact and then go to **20**.

65

The Diver breaks the surface, clutching in one paw a piece of the Great Medallion! Make a note of this, and then go to **20**.

Oh yes, we nearly forgot: well done!

66

Well, using the Builder was a good idea, but unfortunately this is going to be quite a long job. The other Lemmings, never known for sitting around and waiting, soon become restless. Understandably, they want to get to the beach!

After a while, they start to head back along the pier. Now who's going to get there first, the Builder or the Lemmings?

Roll one dice and add the number of Builders in the party to the result. If this number is 8 or more, then go to **217**. If it is 7 or less, then go to **193**.

67

It doesn't take long, and afterwards they feel ready for anything.

Now, which event do you think they should start off with, the javelin (go to **121**) or the pole vault (go to **72**)?

68

What a PAIN! The Miner's pick has struck an iron slab and is broken. There's no getting through this way.

This Lemming is not removed from the party strength, but it may not be used again until we tell you. If this leaves you with no Miners... Oops!

Your adventure ends here

Of course, if you've got lots of them, you can go to **153** and have another go.

69

Ah, a choice of one . . . Go to **61**.

70

Unfortunately the Exploder wanders away from the pillar and achieves nothing. Remove one Exploder from the party strength, and then go back to **11**.

71

The Stackers and Builders don't quite manage to get it quite right. As a result of their labours, the staircase is not only a bit narrow for comfort, it also sways ominously!

Roll one dice. If the result is 3 or more, then go to **136**. If the result is 2 or less, then go to **271**.

72

Ah, the pole vault. Quite a dangerous event, this. Before we go any further though, have the Lemmings 'warmed up'?

If they have, then go to **171**. If they haven't, then go to **304**.

73

The Miner steps up to the pillar and starts to hack away at it with a pickaxe. After several minutes there's not so much as a scratch on it.

Looks like the Lemmings are going to have to try something different. Go back to **11**.

74

The Diggers slog away but are slowed down considerably by the constantly nipping crabs. 'Yeow!'

What a nuisance. The big problem is the incoming tide. If the Diggers don't get a move on, the Lemmings are going to be swamped before they can get through to the centre.

Go to **60**.

75

With military discipline, the Lemmings launch their attack. The Troll swings its club but is thrown off balance before it can strike home. Suddenly the Troll is falling and, with a final yelp, tumbles over the side of the bridge into the river.

'YIPPEE, YIPPEE,' yell the Lemmings.

Triumphantly they stroll across the bridge, laughing at the poor old Troll as it floats harmlessly off downstream.

On the far bank looms the forest! Go to **210**.

76

This looks like just the job for a Builder. He starts to do his thing, while the Attractor keeps the rest of the Lemmings entertained. The job takes quite a while, but in the end the Builder manages to build a bridge that allows the Lemmings to get back to land. Looks like the pier is a no-go area. The Lemmings are going to have to make their way down through the dunes; go to **218**.

77
The Lemmings turn a corner in the path and come face to face with a big pile of rubble. Do they want to try and get rid of the rubble (go to **163**), or will they try another route (go to **259**)?

78
This is the edge of the ice field. To the east stretches the huge polar sea.

Which way do you think the Lemmings should go now: west (go to **110**) or north-west (go to **222**)?

79
You and the Lemmings seem to have switched the engines to full power!

Looks like it's next stop Mars! Anyone for Space Invaders?

Your adventure ends here

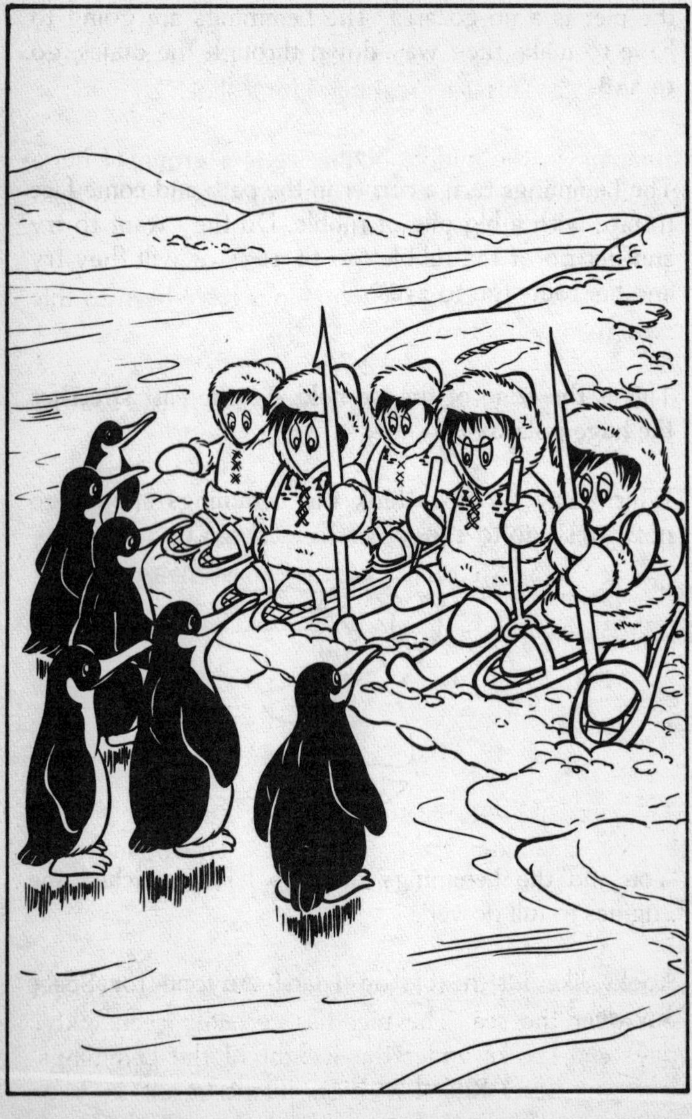

80

After a while, the Lemmings reach an area of very smooth ice. This is a great place for a slide!

Standing in the middle of the ice is a group of huge penguins. They look at the Lemmings for a while, then start to waddle towards them.

If this is the first time the Lemmings have been to this spot, then go to **290**.

If they have been here before, then they may go either south (go to **56**) or south-west (go to **111**).

81

From here the Lemmings can just make out a cave. Inside it is the Medallion and the end of their quest!

Just one obstacle remains . . .

Go to **133**.

82

The pier has been part of the Beach Zone for as long as the Lemmings can remember — which, in truth, isn't all that long. Last Tuesday perhaps, but no longer.

Barbaranne leads the Lemmings down to the pier and out over the sea. The pier has certainly seen better days and creaks under the weight of the Lemmings' tramping feet. Roll one dice. If the result is 3 or less, then go to **176**. If the result is 4 or more, then go to **272**.

83
'RUN AWAY... RUN AWAY!'

The Lemmings scuttle off as fast as they can, but there's no getting away from the Shadow Monster, now that it's on the case. The Lemmings will have to turn and fight it. Go to **165**.

84

The Maze has very narrow paths, and it twists and turns in a most confusing manner. From here, you can carry on in the same direction (go to **178**). Alternatively, you can turn sharp right (go to **57**).

85

The Diggers make short work of the walls, and in no time the Lemmings are deep in the centre of the castle.

Go to **263**.

86

After a few moments, the old spaceship comes to rest on the surface of the strange planet, which is an odd, greyish sort of colour. There are craters everywhere, and now and then the surface bubbles and heaves ominously.

Hmm, a good place for a Space Lemming to be! Go to **162**.

87

Luckily the Exploder goes off right at the edge of the pillar... BOOM!

Remove the Exploder from the party strength, and go to **168**.

88

So how do you suppose the Lemmings are going to get through the wall without a Fencer? Not having one is simply down to bad planning by the brains of the outfit ... and that means *you*!

The Lemmings will have to build some stairs after all, so go to **140**.

89

It's so dark that the Lemmings feel as if they're underground. To keep their spirits up, the Herdman starts to whistle, and soon all the Lemmings are joining in. But they all stop when the path splits to the left and to the right. Which way now? To the left (go to **91**) or to the right (go to **113**)?

90

The Sledgers move to the edge of the slope, and the other Lemmings squeeze in behind them, then it's off down the slope... 'WHEEEEE!'

Go to **220**.

91

The trees tower above the Lemmings, arching over the track so that it looks like an underground tunnel. There is nothing for it but to keep on walking.

Trudging on, go to **211**.

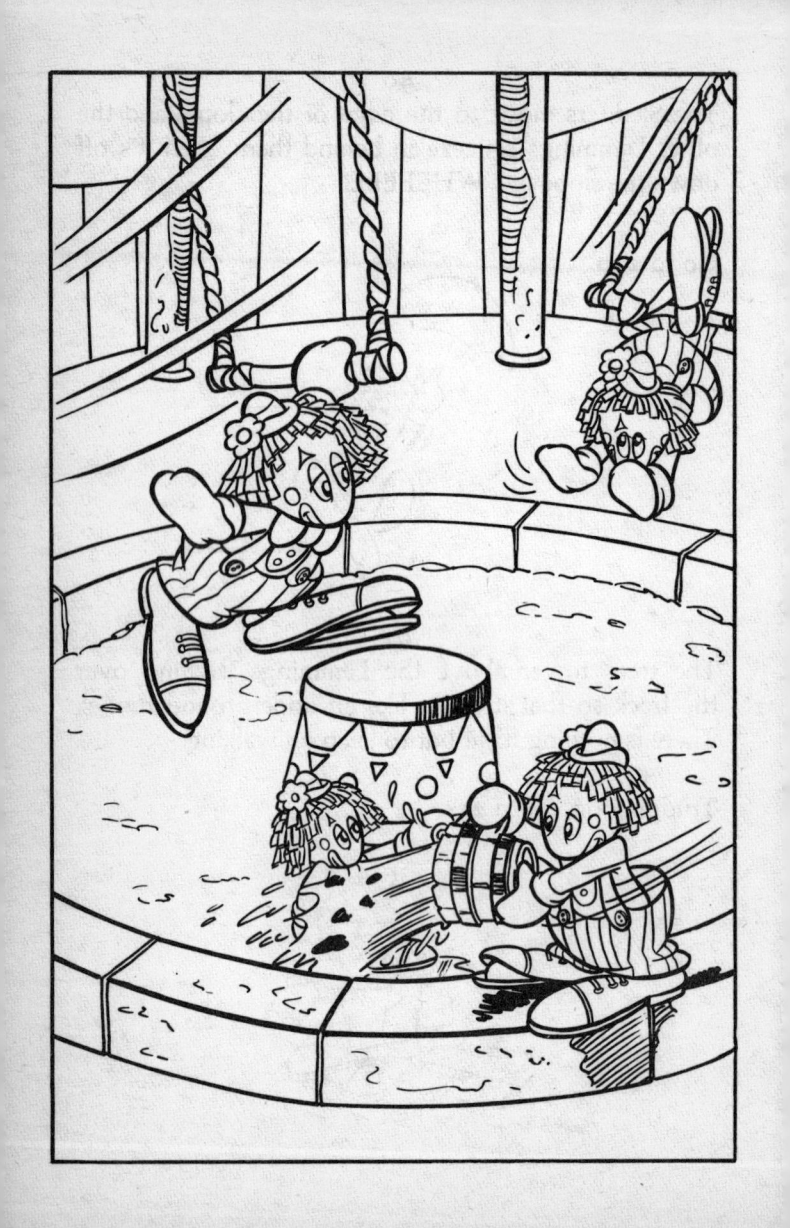

92

The clowns are putting on a great show and they don't seem to mind the Lemmings joining in! Unfortunately, one or two of the Lemmings are getting

so involved that they seem to have forgotten all about the quest. Go to **367**.

93

The Lemmings turn a corner in the path and come face to face with a big pile of rubble.

Do the Lemmings want to try and get rid of the rubble (go to **50**), or will they try another route (go to **229**)?

94

Before they can even start this part of the quest for the Medallion, the Shadow Lemmings are going to have to get through the Shadow Maze. This is a ghastly place ... go to **5**.

95

The Lemmings fight hard but the monster gets the better of them. One poor Lemming gets eaten! (This monster is truly OUT OF ORDER!)

What will the Lemmings do now? They can always give the monster the THRASHING IT DESERVES!! (We're trying to motivate you here!) In this case, go to **165**. Or will they be lily-livered cowardy custards and run away (go to **83**)?

96

This seems like a good idea. It isn't that far to build – but if a Lemming should fall, that lion down there does look awfully hungry! Go to **140**.

97

The pit doesn't look too wide, so perhaps the Lemmings could jump across . . .

Roll one dice. If the score is 3 or more, then go to **194**. If the result is 2 or less, then go to **232**.

98

Despite all their efforts, the Lemmings are beaten back by the Troll, who simply swats them like flies.

Work out the difference between the Lemmings' dice roll and the Troll's. This is the number of brave Lemmings who have been slain by the wicked Troll. Remove that number (you choose which) from the party.

The Troll stands and laughs at the defeated Lemmings.

There's nothing for it now but to try to cross the river somewhere else. Go to **315**.

99

The Maze has very narrow paths and it twists and turns in a most confusing manner. These are the options open to you now: you can turn right (go to **107**), turn sharp left (go to **178**) or choose an in-between route (go to **249**).

100

At last! The Lemmings have reached 'X marks the spot', but where's the Medallion? It should have been right here. Barbaranne looks confused. The tide is almost in, and all there is in the centre of the sandcastle is a little rock pool.

What do you want to do: have a think about it (go to **358**) or let a Diver take a look in the pool (go to **399**)?

101

The Blocker stands right next to the pillar – and there it stays, just as you would expect!

Hmm ... what now? If you fancy using an Exploder, go to **29**. If you prefer to try something else, go to **11**.

102

Without a second (or, for that matter a first) thought, Buzz pulls the green lever. A disembodied voice announces: 'Auto pilot on', and the spaceship starts to slowly move down towards the planet.

Good guess! Go to **86**.

103

Well, if this comes off, then it's going to give the Lemmings a big advantage.

Roll one dice. If the result is 4 or more, then go to **241**. If the result is 3 or less, then go to **308**.

104

No problem at all! Well, not strictly true, but in the final analysis the Lemmings all make it across to the other side. It was a bit wobbly in the middle, but no one fell off! Now go to **281**.

105

What a PAIN! The Miner's pick has struck an iron slab and now is broken. There's no getting through this way.

This Lemming is not removed from the party strength, but it may not be used again until we tell you. If this leaves you with no Miners ... Oops!

Your adventure ends here

Of course, if you've got lots of them, you can go to **243** and have another go.

106

Quite wisely, the Shadow Lemmings (who, you should remember, live permanently in the dark) walk away from the light, followed by the rest of the party. After a short walk along the passage, they come to a large pit in the floor. If there is a Roper in the party, you may go to **117**. If there isn't one, then go to **97**.

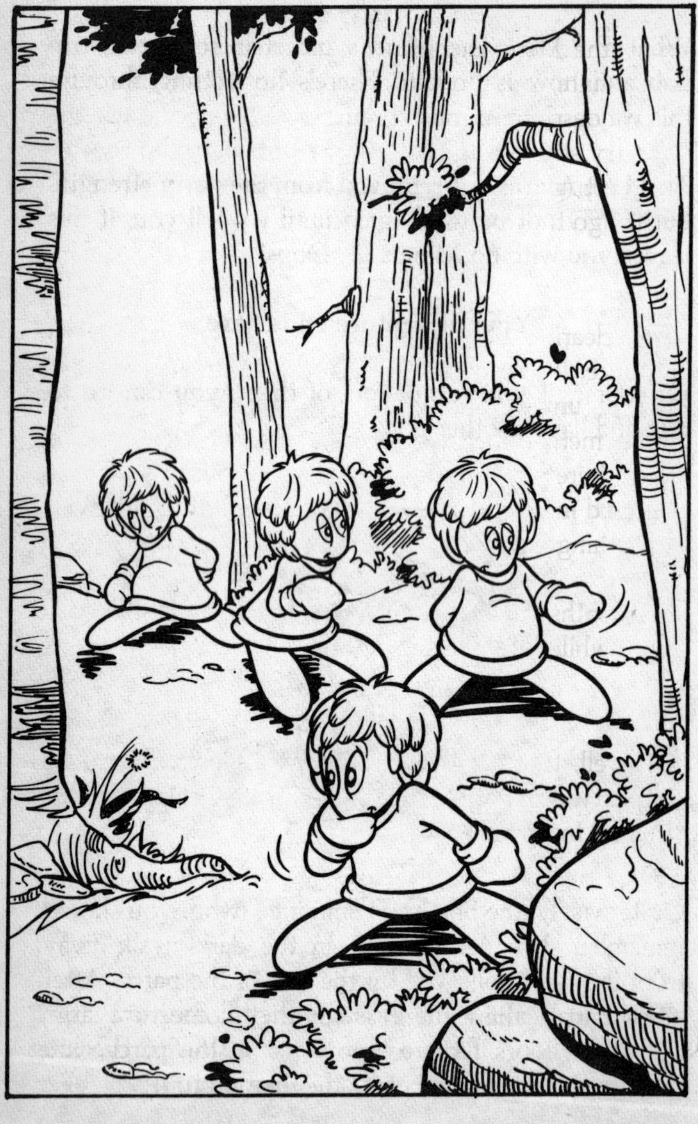

107

Now the Lemmings have reached a crossroads; they seem quite happy about this, so why aren't you? After all, it doesn't take much brain power to decide whether to carry straight on (go to **392**), turn right (go to **363**), turn left (go to **249**) or go back the way you've just come (go to **99**).

108

The clearing soon disappears behind them in the distance. It's so dark now that the Lemmings feel as if they're underground. The trail continues for a few more metres then opens into another clearing. The floor here is carpeted with small bushes that are covered in bright red berries that smell of ... phew ... something bad!

Two paths leave the clearing. One goes south (go to **397**); while the other goes west (go to **113**).

109

Ah well, that's it then. Looks like the Sporting Lemmings weren't quite up to the job. Or was it their trainer? In any event ...

Your adventure ends here

110

This part of the ice field is covered in deep crevasses. The Lemmings have to move very slowly, checking each piece of ground before they tread on it.

Roll one dice. If the result is 4 or more, then the Lemmings may either go to the south (go to **340**) or head west (go to **56**).

If the result of the dice roll is 3 or less, then go to **245**.

111

The Lemmings have reached the western edge of the ice field. To the west towers a huge range of mountains. You don't want to go that way!

So which way should they go: north (go to **196**) or north-west (go to **373**)?

112

The Builder starts to build – but unfortunately there isn't enough room for the Builder to work properly and in the end the Lemmings have to give up.

If there is a Glue Pourer in the party, then go to **41**.

... otherwise it's your-adventure-ends-here time!

113

The path winds through the trees, gradually making its way uphill until the Lemmings find themselves at the top of a small hillock. The forest stretches out beneath them in all directions as far as the eye can see. And still there is not a sign of Castle Hollow to be seen.

Two tracks lead down from the hillock, one to the south and one off to the west. Which one will they follow, the one going south (go to **40**) or the one going west (go to **91**)?

114

The Lemmings turn on the tap, and out pours a funny-smelling liquid that the Flame Throwers seem to recognize. Congratulations, you've found a refill for the Flame Throwers; all of them that were used in the maze are now back in working order. Make a note of this fact, and then it's time to go down those stairs, so go to **342**.

(The sign said: 'CAUTION INFLAMMABLE' by the way!)

115

The tunnel goes still deeper! Which way now? Should it move to the left (go to **285**) or to the right (go to **174**)?

116

No, just kidding. It is in actual fact just another bit of maze. From here the Lemmings can either go off to the left (go to **299**) or they can carry straight on (go to **317**).

117

Just the job for a Roper. In no time a safety line is stretched across the pit and soon all the Lemmings are across. Go to **318**.

The Polar Lemmings' village is shrouded in a thick blanket of snow and, since the Lemming houses are no more than igloos made out of ice anyway, it's almost invisible.

Captain Scottemming, the village's head Lemming, stands at the front of the party and looks up at the sky. 'Blizzard comes,' he says, looking at the grey clouds. 'Let's go!'

'Let's go!' shout the other Lemmings.

Before you continue, you must decide which Lemmings are going to be in the party. How many can you have depends on the number of Lemmings you finished the last zone with. Simply trade in the Lemmings you have for the new ones listed below, on a one-for-one basis. If this is the first zone you have visited, then you may choose 50 Lemmings.

Lemmings available in the Polar Zone

Skater	Sledger	Skier
Roller	Attractor	Slider
Thrower	Scooper	Kayaker

Once you have chosen your Lemmings, it's into the ice field that surrounds the Polar Lemmings' village ... but which direction?

South, go to **250**.

West, go to **126**.

East, go to **146**.

119

Right then, let's go!

The Lemmings know that they have to get to a particular part of the beach. 'X' marks the spot, you might say. Once they've found it, all they have to do is dig, and their part of the Medallion should be found. Sounds simple, doesn't it? We'll see!

There are two ways to get down to the beach from the club. The Lemmings can either go through the dunes (go to **218**) or make their way down to the pier (go to **82**).

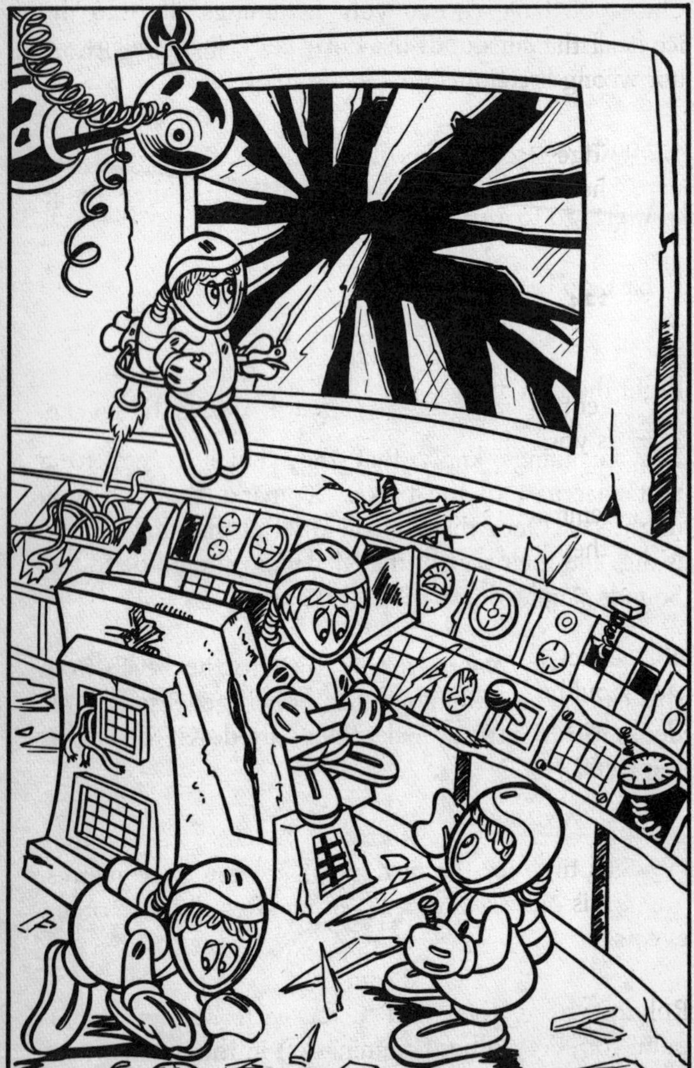

120

Now all that mess is out of the way, it's just a short walk along the corridor to the bridge.

The bridge itself is almost as tatty as the rest of the ship. There are dozens of odd-looking machines lying around.

Go to **224**.

121

This event is quite straightforward: throw the javelin as far as you can!

If the Lemmings have already 'warmed up', then go to **247**. If they haven't, then go to **372**.

122

The tunnel must break through soon. In which direction should the tunnellers head now? Should they carry on in the same direction (go to **154**) or veer off to the left (go to **115**)?

123

Now it's time for the final event. It's the 1500 metres — which is quite a long way to run after all those other events.

Roll one dice, then add 3 for each Runner and 1 point for every other Lemming left in the party. Make a note of this score, and then go to **198**.

124

Roll one dice. If the result is 4 or more, go to **87**. If the result is 3 or less, then go to **70**.

125

It was a good idea to use the Skiers, but there just weren't enough of them. Halfway down the slope, a Lemming trips and turns into a Roller without really meaning to! By the time he comes to a stop, three more Lemmings have been trapped in a huge snowball. It'll take far too long to dig them out, so you'll have to leave them behind. Remove four Lemmings of your choice from the party, and then go to **220**.

126

The Lemmings bravely set out into the ice field. Unfortunately, it's summer at the moment — not that you'd know it — but the weather is still warm enough to have melted some of the ice.

The ice field is a very dangerous place.

Which way will the Lemmings go now: to the west (go to **246**) or to the east (go to **48**)?

127

The Lemmings will score points depending on how well they do in each event ... and what do points mean? Medals! To win the Medallion, the Lemmings are going to need lots of medals!

The games will start soon. What do you want the Lemmings to do now: go for a short run to 'warm up' (go to **261**) or go to the javelin event (go to **121**) or the pole vault event (go to **72**)?

128

The Lemmings are very near the Medallion now. It should be just round the next bend. Go to **223**.

129

You and the Lemmings seem to have switched the engines on to full power!

Luckily for you, the spaceship happened to be pointing the right way!

So off you zoom. Go to **86**.

130

Oh well, what does an odd risk or two matter to a Circus Lemming? Up they climb, one after another, then start to edge out across the swaying rope. Go to **313**.

131

The Herdman steps forward and bows deeply to the Troll. Then the Herdman gestures towards the other side of the river. The Troll glances at the Herdman, then he gazes at the rest of the Lemmings for a few moments with a vacant look on his face.

'Erm ... all right then,' he says at last.

As quickly as they can, the Lemmings scuttle across the bridge until they reach the far side safely.

'Phew!'

Go to **210**.

132

The first obstacle the Lemmings need to negotiate is a circus ring full of tumbling clowns.

What will the Lemmings do? They could always try to walk across the tightrope that is suspended above the clowns – be warned, it's a long way off the ground! If this is what you want them to do, go to **130**.

Having inspected them though, the clowns actually look quite friendly. The Lemmings could always try just walking straight among them. If this is your preference, go to **92**.

133

The hole in the platform is wide, but it isn't very deep.

How will the Lemmings get round this one? Will they use Builders (go to **157**) or Fillers (go to **59**)?

134

Oh NO! The Lemmings have stepped on the start-line and been disqualified! Well, if you will take these chances . . .

If the Lemmings haven't already competed in, or been disqualified from the triple jump, then they may go to **167**.

Otherwise, go to **273**.

135

The Basher steps up and takes a mighty swing at the pillar.

'CLANG!!!'

The Basher's club bounces off, sending the poor Basher several metres through the air, to land with a thud on the platform.

Looks like you'd better think of something else – go back to **11**.

136

Despite the rickety staircase, the Lemmings still manage to get across and over the lion. Go to **378**.

137

The barrel does indeed have a tap on the side of it. There is also a big sign at the side of it saying: 'C TI N I FL   MA   E'... The sign is a bit old and some of the letters have fallen off. What can it mean?

Do you want the Lemmings to turn on the tap (go to **114**)?

If you think it would be safer for them just to go down the stairs, then go to **342**.

138

While the judges are working out the scores, you may compete in the pole vault if the Lemmings have not already done so. Go to **72**.

If the Lemmings *have* already competed in the pole vault or have been told that they cannot, then go to **169**.

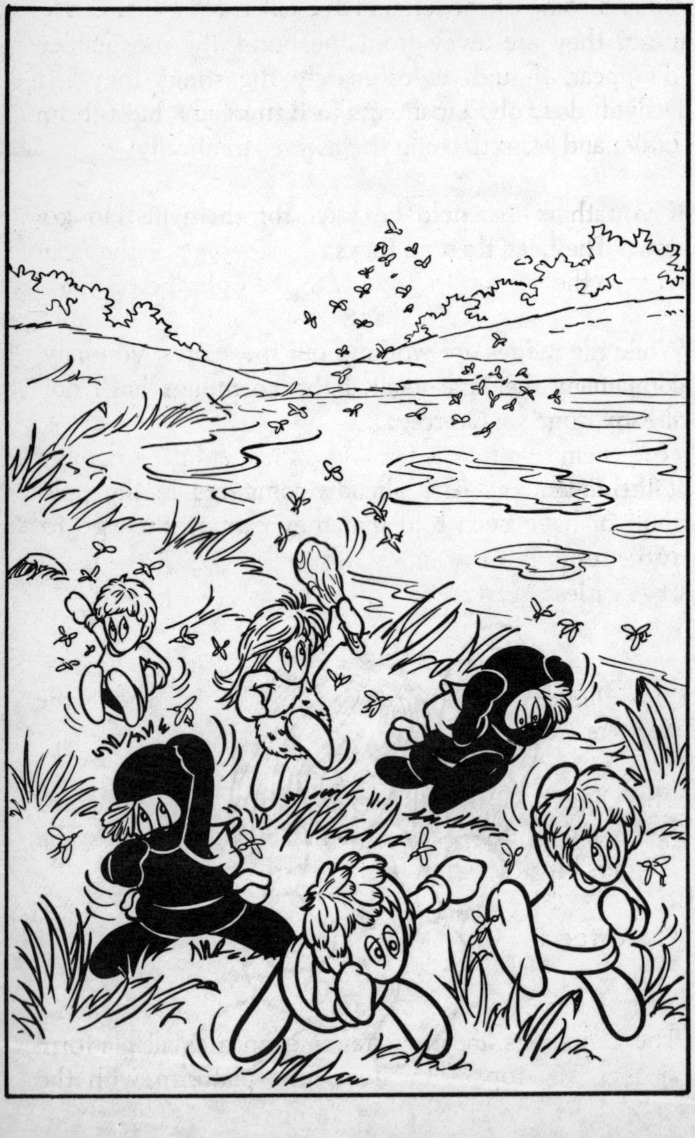

139

Once they are away from the pond, the mosquitoes disappear, though unfortunately the stings they left behind do not! Most of the Lemmings have been bitten and are scratching themselves frantically!

The path splits into three. Which way will they go now? They can go straight on (go to **375**); or they can veer to the left (go to **397**), or to the right (go to **319**).

140

How many Builders and Stackers are in the party?

Add them up and then roll one dice. Add the number rolled to the total of Builders and Stackers.

If the result is 12 or more, then go to **274**. If the result is 11 or less, then go to **71**.

141

The Diggers dig, the crabs nip. 'Yeow!' shout the Diggers.

The Diggers dig some more, and the crabs nip some more, and so it goes on until, against all the odds, the Diggers break through to the centre of the tower.

Go to **100**.

142

The Lemmings are now standing on a small platform at the very top of the tent. The platform with the

Medallion can now clearly be seen. There's just one smallish gap to get across.

How are the Lemmings going to do this? If you want them to use a Builder, go to **112**. If you think a Glue Pourer is right for the job, go to **41**.

143
OK then, which way now? To the left (go to **36**) or to the right (go to **260**)?

144
All the Lemmings jump off the comet.

Hmm, now what? Float around in space for a thousand years, we would think . . .

Your adventure ends here

145
Swimmers, huh? Let's think now. Rock pool, full of water, Swimmers. Yes, that seems to work out OK!

The Swimmers make it across the pool and lower the ready-made bridge. The other Lemmings march across the bridge . . . and that's about it really. Easy when you do it right, isn't it!

Now go to **34**.

146

The Lemmings bravely set out into the ice field. Unfortunately, it's summer at the moment — not that you'd know it — but the weather is still warm enough to have melted some of the ice.

The ice field is now a very dangerous place.

Which way will the Lemmings go now: to the west (go to **225**) or to the east (go to **286**)?

147

What a shambles! There are Lemmings everywhere! All covered in snow and ice. If that's the best you can come up with, then perhaps the Lemmings are better off on their own!

Roll one dice and remove that number of Lemmings from the party. We'll let you choose which ones to lose, just to be nice to you — though you don't really even deserve that. Now go to **220** — at least some of the Lemmings have reached the bottom!

148

The Lemmings march triumphantly through the tunnel the Basher has just made.

Oh NO! Only a short way ahead is a wide chasm. These are usually bottomless and always fatal! What's more, the Lemmings are marching straight towards it.

Go to **155**.

149

The path gets even narrower as it enters the forest. It's so dark that the Lemmings have to strain their eyes to see even a few metres in front of them. This is not a nice place!

After a few hundred metres, the path forks again.

Which way will the Lemmings go now? To the right? Go to **12**. To the left? Go to **151**.

150

The Lemmings walk straight towards the light, which grows brighter and brighter. Eventually it gets so bright that the poor Lemmings are dazzled and blinded. Their eyes just aren't used to such a bright light!

The Lemmings' sight *will* come back, but not for a while. For now, they're going to have to stumble around blind! Go to **172**.

151

The Lemmings march slowly along the footpath, only the regular tramp of their feet disturbing the silence of the forest.

After a while the path disappears into a tangle of trees and thorn bushes. Oh dear! Which way will they go now? Will they turn left (go to **248**) or will they go to the right (go to **108**)?

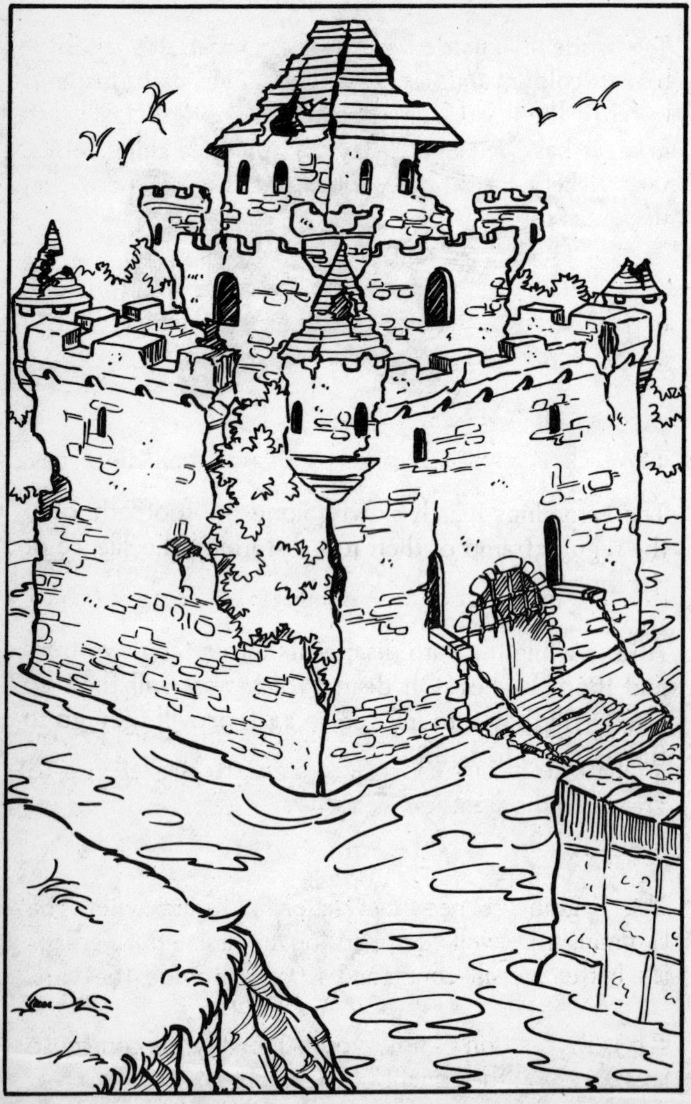

152

The castle is guarded by a wide moat. It's a dirty brown colour and smells awful! The path leading towards the castle ends at a drawbridge. Like the moat, it has seen better days! The whole thing looks very rickety, with holes here and there where the wood has rotted away.

How will the Lemmings cross the moat? They could use the drawbridge (go to **264**), or they could try getting across some other way (go to **239**).

153

The rock is nice and soft, and soon the Miner has constructed quite a deep tunnel.

What now? Do you want to carry on in the same direction (go to **206**) or turn a little to the right (go to **287**)?

154

The tunnel goes still deeper! Which direction do you want to go in now? Will you move to the left (go to **174**) or to the right (go to **213**)?

155

This is going to need fast action and quick wits. The Lemmings are well equipped for the first — but perhaps it's better for all concerned if you provide the wits.

(Or is it? We don't know you personally, of course, so let's give you the benefit of the doubt!)

If you want a Builder to try constructing a bridge, go to **377**. Alternatively, you could use a Blocker to hold up the party and give the Lemmings a little more time (go to **212**).

156

The snowfield goes on for what seems like ages: just a huge expanse of flat snow. A bit boring, really. Anyway, at long last another range of hills comes into view — and there in the side of one of them is a cave!

Go to **291**.

157

The hole is a bit wide for Builders.

How many Builders are in the party? If there are 5 or more, then go to **233**. If there are less than 5, then go to **207**.

158

The Lemmings wait, poised at the end of the platform, as the comet approaches, and at just the right moment they all leap aboard.

Success, so go to **19**.

159

The Ropers take aim at the spaceship. It's a big target, but the Lemmings on the comet are moving very fast ... They're only going to get one chance at this!

Go to **188**.

160

The tunnel is going like a dream.

Where should the tunnellers head for now? Should they carry on the same way (go to **14**) or turn a little to the left (go to **396**)?

161

Congratulations! The Lemmings have reached the top of the mast and found their part of the Medallion!

Make a note of this fact, and then go to **20**.

162

Now that they've landed, the Lemmings find themselves only a short walk from the disused space station, and – just for a change – there are no nasty obstacles in their way.

The space station is the usual type of thing: you know, domes and pods, but unfortunately the Medallion is hidden right at the top of the station's radio mast which, to say the least, is rather tall!

Looks like a mountaineering mission is on the cards. Go to **199**.

163

A Flame Thrower will be able to get rid of the rubble easily. Unfortunately, each Flame Thrower can be used only once. If the Flame Thrower is used, you may remove the rubble and then go to **69**.

If you decide to do this, make a note that one Flame Thrower is now 'out of fuel'. You'd best be careful here since, as we have already told you, there's no guarantee that the rubble won't be back again if the Lemmings retrace their steps!

If you think the Lemmings should simply retrace their steps and try another path, then go to **259**.

164

The Ropers panic and, although some of the ropes hit the target, there's nowhere near enough for the rest of the Lemmings to get across. There's just enough time to use a Jet Pack Lemming; if you have one, go to **280**.

Otherwise it's . . .

your-adventure-ends-here time!

165

This is how to fight the Shadow Monster. Add together all of the Flame Throwers in the party who still have fuel and score 1 point for each. Next, add up all the Archers and Bombers, and score ½ a point for each. Finally, add up all of the rest and score ¼ of a point for each. (Better than a maths lesson, this!) Round any fractions down, so that 8¾ would be counted as 8. This number is the Lemmings' fighting score. The Shadow Monster's fighting score is 11.

Now roll one dice and add the result to the Lemmings' fighting score. If this number is 11 or more, then go to **175**. If the number is 10 or less, then go to **95**.

166

From here the Lemmings can take either a straight path (go to **36**), or a gently curving one (go to **186**).

167

The triple jump is a sort of 'hop, skip and a jump' kind of thing. The general idea is to get as far as you can using just one hop, one skip and then one jump. The Lemmings will have to begin their hop before they hit the start-line. Obviously, they want to get as near to it as possible — but if they tread on it, then they get disqualified!

What do you think they should do: play it safe (go to **254**) or take a chance (go to **103**)?

168

When the dust has cleared, there's a hole in the pillar!

'Yippee!' The Lemmings march triumphantly through.

Go to **45**.

169

Well, that's the end of the first round of the Games; the medal ceremonies are about to start. Do you want the Lemmings to go to the medal ceremony (go to **386**) or head for the next round of events (go to **237**)?

170

Triumphantly, the Lemmings dive into the cave and collect the Medallion.

'YIPPEE!!'

Make a note of this fact, and then go to **20**.

Well done!

171

The Pole Vaulter charges towards the jump and then leaps up the pole for all it's worth...

Go to 24.

172

The Lemmings stumble along. They're not quite comfortable, but nothing bad has happened yet.

Go to 348 or go to 31.

173

Welcome to the Sports Zone. This is the home of the Mega-fit Lemmings — you know the sort: all tracksuits and 'Wash and Go'.

This is the start of the Sports Zone. Before you go any further, you must select the Lemmings that will go on this part of the quest. How many you can have depends on the number of Lemmings you finished the last zone with. Simply trade in the Lemmings you already have for the new ones listed below on a one-for-one basis. If this is the first zone you have visited, then you may choose 50 Lemmings.

Lemmings available in the Sports Zone
Jumper	Runner	Hopper
Swimmer	Spearer	Pole Vaulter
Diver	Archer	Roper

Once you have done this, make a note of the ones you have chosen, then go to **251**.

174

At last, the Miner breaks through. The Lemmings are right above a pool of bubbling water.

The only way out of this is to use Builders. If you haven't got any it's — yes you've guessed it —

Your adventure ends here

If you have, then go to **18**.

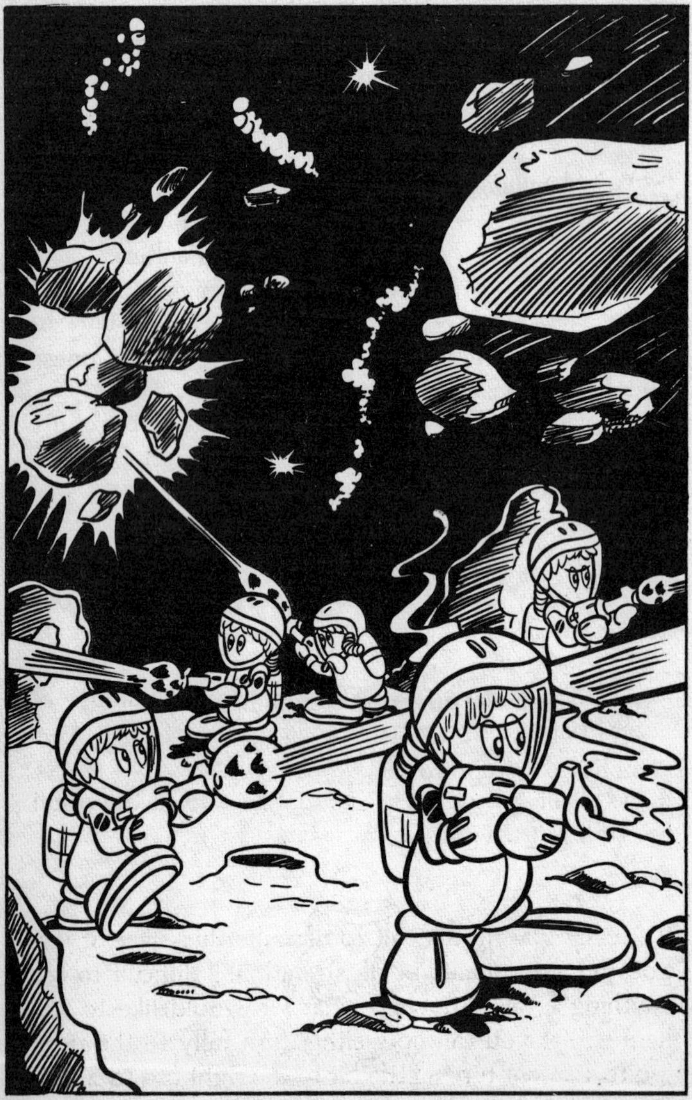

175

Congratulations! The Lemmings have beaten off the Shadow Monster, who runs away, yelping. Smart one, Lemmings!

Now go to **54**.

176

Oh NO! Just as the Lemmings reach almost to the end of the pier, it finally gives up the ghost and starts to collapse under their feet.

Most of them manage to scrabble to safety, but sadly two of them fall into the sea and are lost (remove two Lemmings of your choice from the party).

Now go to **235**.

177

The Laser Blasters take aim at the asteroid and fire. Roll one dice and add the result to the number of Laser Blasters in the party.

If the result is 8 or more, then go to **338**. If the result is 7 or less, then go to **276**.

178

It's really getting difficult to describe this maze: it just goes on and on and, being so dark, it's difficult to see anything at all. Anyway, what we would like to say here is that you can now either turn fully to the right (go to **249**), or turn a little bit to the right (go to **201**).

179

The Lemmings follow the stairs down and find themselves on a flat platform. To the left, a huge iron wall looms up into the clouds. Can't go that way. To the right, there is a large hill.

Go to **289**.

180

The Lemmings wait, poised, as the comet approaches. The Ropers aim and then fire.

Success!
The remaining Lemmings grab hold of the ropes and drag themselves on to the speeding comet and, believe it or not, they all make it aboard!

Go to **19**.

181

The path grows even narrower as it enters the forest. It's so dark that the Lemmings have to strain their eyes to see even a few metres in front of them. This is not a nice place!

After a few hundred metres, the path forks again. Which way will the Lemmings go now, to the right (go to **248**) or to the left (go to **211**)?

182
BOOM, and the Lemming sails through the air in a perfect arc, to land on the platform high above. One after another, all the other Lemmings follow ... Go to **142**.

183
Not wanting to be disqualified, the Lemmings decide to take off well before the start-line, though this means that the jump isn't going to be as long as it might have been. Go to **273**.

184
What a surprise – more snow, more ice ...

Which way now: south-west (go to **222**) or south-east (go to **7**)?

185

The Lemmings now find themselves in the courtyard of the castle. All around stand or lie the rotting remains of a once magnificent building. Here and there are large piles of rubble, and the whole place looks decidedly dangerous. A great place for Lemmings to hang out in, as a matter of fact!

The Herdman looks around for a few moments then he points towards a large pile of rubble in the far corner. 'Let's go!'

How will the Lemmings get through the rubble? You can use a Miner (go to **226**) or a Basher (go to **296**) or another Lemming (go to **360**).

Remember that you *must* have a suitable Lemming in the party before you can choose that option. If, for example, you don't have any Miners you *cannot* choose the Miner option.

186

This is a three-way junction. Lucky you! Now you can go to the left (go to **322**), to the right (go to **389**) or follow the middle path (go to **302**).

187

At least the Lemmings can feel their way along the wall of the passageway ... walking towards that light was really a dumb idea!

Go to either **30** or **265**.

188

Roll one dice and add the result to the number of Ropers in the party.

If this adds up to 7 or more, then go to **236**. If the result is 6 or less, then go to **164**.

189

Is there a Fencer in the party? If there is, then go to **282**. If there isn't, then go to **88**.

190

When the dust has cleared, there's a hole in the pillar!

'Yippee.' The Lemmings march through. (Remember to remove a Blocker and an Exploder from the party – still, it's what they would have wanted!)

Go to **45**.

191

Despite frantic efforts, four Lemmings tumble in for an early bath (remove four Lemmings of your choice from the party). At least the other Lemmings are across — but is it a case of 'out of the frying pan and into the fire'?

Go to **46**.

192

To do this, you're going to have to do some adding up.
If you chose 'High' on the lever, score 3 points; if you chose 'Med', score 2; and if you chose 'Low', score 1.

Now have a look at what you chose on the dial.

If you chose 'Bang', score 1 point; if you chose 'Boom', score 2 points; and if you chose 'You Sure?', score 3 points.

Add the two scores together. If they come to 5 or more, then go to **182**. If they come to 4 or less, then go to **62**.

193

The Builder made it eventually, but, oh dear! The Lemmings were in such a hurry that three of them have gone for a swim, without really meaning to. The water is great and sadly there is NO chance of getting them out. Remove three Lemmings of your choice from the party. There's nothing for it now but to go back and make your way through the dunes. Go to **218**.

194
Yes, that wasn't too difficult. In a short while, the Lemmings are all safely across the pit.

Now go to **318**.

195
'Surf's up!' shout the Surfers, and it's on with the shades and out with the boards for these cool dudes.

Sadly, there's one small flaw in this plan: NO SURF. This is a rock pool, or hadn't you noticed! The Surfers realize this too late, and the first Surfer sinks to the bottom of the pool, never to be seen again (remove one Surfer from the party).

Now go back to **270** and try something else.

196
It's very quiet out here. Only the sound of the Lemmings' feet and the distant howling of the wind break the silence.

Which way will the Lemmings head now: south (go to **111**) or will they turn south-west (go to **373**)?

197
Unfortunately, because the Pole Vaulter hadn't warmed up, it manages to pull a muscle in the first round!

Remove the Pole Vaulter from the party strength and make a note that the Lemmings may not compete in the Pole Vault again! Go to **261**.

198

The thing about the pentathlon is that the Lemmings need to have done well in nearly all the events to stand a chance of winning a medal.

The judges study their score-sheets intently and start to fiddle with calculators and stop-watches.

Go to **39**.

199

The radio mast spears up in to the sky. There used to be a lift ages ago — but of course it's broken now.

How are the Lemmings going to get to the top and collect the Medallion? Are they going to use a Roper (go to **262**) or Magno Boots (go to **393**)?

200

The pool looms in front of the marching Lemmings, who of course carry on marching towards it with gay abandon — after all, what else would you expect?

Is there a Blocker in the party? If there is and you want to use it, then you'd better go to **257**. If you don't have a Blocker or if you don't want to use it, then go to **215**.

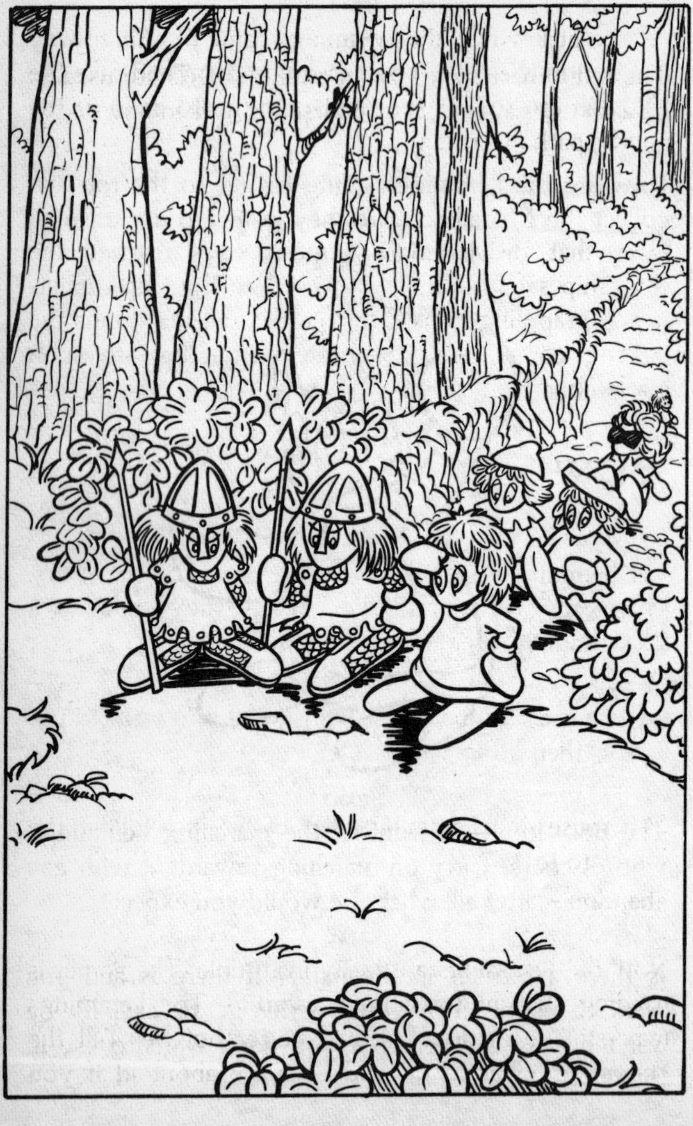

201

After a little while, the Lemmings come to a three-way junction in the path. You can guide them and take the left path (go to **36**), the right path (go to **260**) or the middle path (go to **23**).

202

Now that the Jet Pack Lemming has reached the spaceship safely, it's easy to activate the ship's emergency grappling hook. This reaches out and grabs the passing comet, and the other Lemmings are soon safely aboard.

Go to **351**.

203

The Lemmings set off, marching towards the stairs. They only get a short way before they come to a small landing where the stairs turn a corner.

If there is a Stomper in the party, and you want to use it here, then go to **55**.

Otherwise, the Lemmings had better just follow the stairs; go to **179**.

204

Now the Lemmings are really in trouble. The comet is heading straight for a huge asteroid. The Lemmings may still be in doubt. You'd better not be! Tell the Lemmings what to do and be quick about it! If you want them to use a Laser Blaster, go to **244**. If you think a Super Lem! will be of any use, go to **298**.

205

The Climber zips up the face of the hill and over the other side in an instant. If you have a Basher in the party, he can now get helped over the hill, and it will be easy to bash through from this side, so go to **148**.

If there aren't any Bashers, then we're afraid . . .

Your adventure ends here!

206

The tunnel is going like a dream.

The Lemmings need to carry on digging though, so which way now? Shall they carry on in the same direction (go to **344**) or turn a little to the left (go to **295**)?

207

No, it's no good. The hole is just too wide for the Builders in the party. Looks like the Lemmings will have to go back to **133** and try something else.

208

The judges carefully measure out the distances of each throw.

It's a tense moment!

Go to **138**.

209

Unfortunately, because the Spearer wasn't warmed up, it manages to pull a muscle in the first round! Remove the Spearer from the party strength and make a note that the Lemmings may not compete in the javelin event again! Go to **261**.

210

The narrow, overgrown path looks as if it hasn't been trodden for many years — not surprisingly, for it leads through the forest.

The forest looms up, dark and menacing, before the brave Lemmings.

The place has a faint, musty smell that causes the Lemmings' noses to twitch like rabbits'. Just as the path enters the first clumps of wizened oaks, it splits in two.

Which path will the Lemmings follow? If they choose the right one, go to **149**. If they like the look of the left one, go to **181**.

211

The path curves slowly to the left then back to the right again. Only the crunching of the Lemmings' feet breaks the deathly silence.

After five minutes or so, the Lemmings find the path blocked by a thorny thicket. What will they do now? They can either turn to the right (go to **248**) or push on towards the left (go to **89**).

212

Just what was needed! The Blocker zooms ahead of the party and does its stuff.

Go to **242**.

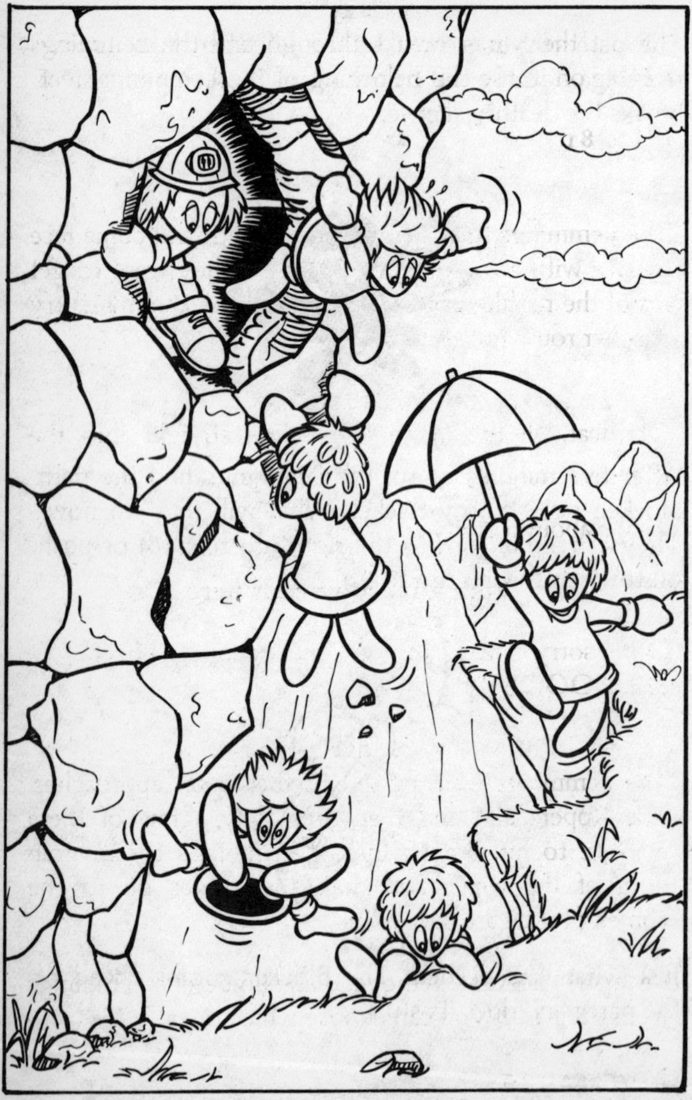

213

At last the Miner breaks through and the Lemmings tumble on to the cliff below.

Go to **81**.

214

The Lemmings turn a corner in the path and come face to face with a big pile of rubble. Do they want to get rid of the rubble (go to **389**), or will the Lemmings try another route (go to **229**)?

215

Oh dear, all the Lemmings march straight into the pool.

That's about it really . . .

Your adventure ends here

Oh, sorry, we forgot the sound effect . . . SPLOOOOSH!!!

216

The Lemmings wait, poised, as the comet approaches. The Ropers aim and then fire. Only a few of them manage to hit. Frantically the Lemmings try to grab hold of the ropes and drag themselves on to the comet. Not all are successful.

Roll one dice and remove that number of Lemmings from the party (you can choose which ones).

Now go to **19**.

217

Well, that was a close-run thing, but somehow the Builder just managed to keep in front of the impatient Lemmings, and all make it safely back to land. There's nothing for it now but to head down through the dunes. Go to **218**.

218

The Lemmings set off towards the dunes. Because they're constantly being blown about by the wind, the dunes are always changing shape. As you might have guessed, a huge one is now blocking the Lemmings' path.

How will they get over it? They can use Diggers (go to **343**) or Runners (go to **330**).

219

The Lemmings are taken back outside, into the grassy bit in the middle of the track. There's a pole balanced on two pieces of wood in front of them, about one and a half metres off the ground. Choose the Lemmings for this game now, and then go to **52**.

220

So here we are, then. One way or another, the Lemmings have reached the bottom of the hill.

From here the Lemmings have a choice. Do they walk towards a snowfield (go to **156**)? Or will they make for a frozen lake (go to **238**)?

221

The bridge is the most direct route, so the bridge it's going to be! Defiantly the Lemmings stride on to the bridge, led by the Herdman. They are almost halfway across before anything happens. Go to **63**.

222

It's just as well that the Polar Lemmings are used to the cold. It's freezing out here!

Which way now: west (go to **80**) or south-east (go to **78**)?

223

Oh no, there's more rubble!

The Lemmings can see the Medallion glinting behind the obstacle, but it's just out of reach. The only way to get it is to burn away the rubble with a Flame Thrower.

If you have one of these in the party and he still has fuel left, then go to **27**. If there isn't one, go to **51**.

224

The Lemmings must somehow get the spaceship to take them down to the planet's surface; it comes down to a choice of three things — which is just as well, since we don't think either you or the Lemmings could cope with any more!

What do you think they should do? If you reckon they should press the black button marked 'Eugh!', go to **279**. If the green lever marked 'Yippee!' takes your fancy, go to **252**. If you think twisting the red dial marked 'Oops!' will do any good, go to **21**.

225

As far as the eye can see, everything is a pure, dazzling white. The odd flake of snow is beginning to fall, too. Best that the Lemmings hurry!

Will they go east (go to **286**) or south-east (go to **7**)?

226

The Miner steps up to the rubble, spits on his paws, rubs them together and sets about the rock with enthusiasm. In no time at all a tunnel appears, and the rest of the Lemmings follow the Miner and the Herdman into it. Go to **345**.

227

Well, if this comes off, then it's going to give the Lemmings a big advantage.

Roll one dice. If the result is 4 or more, then go to **268**. If the result is 3 or less, then go to **134**.

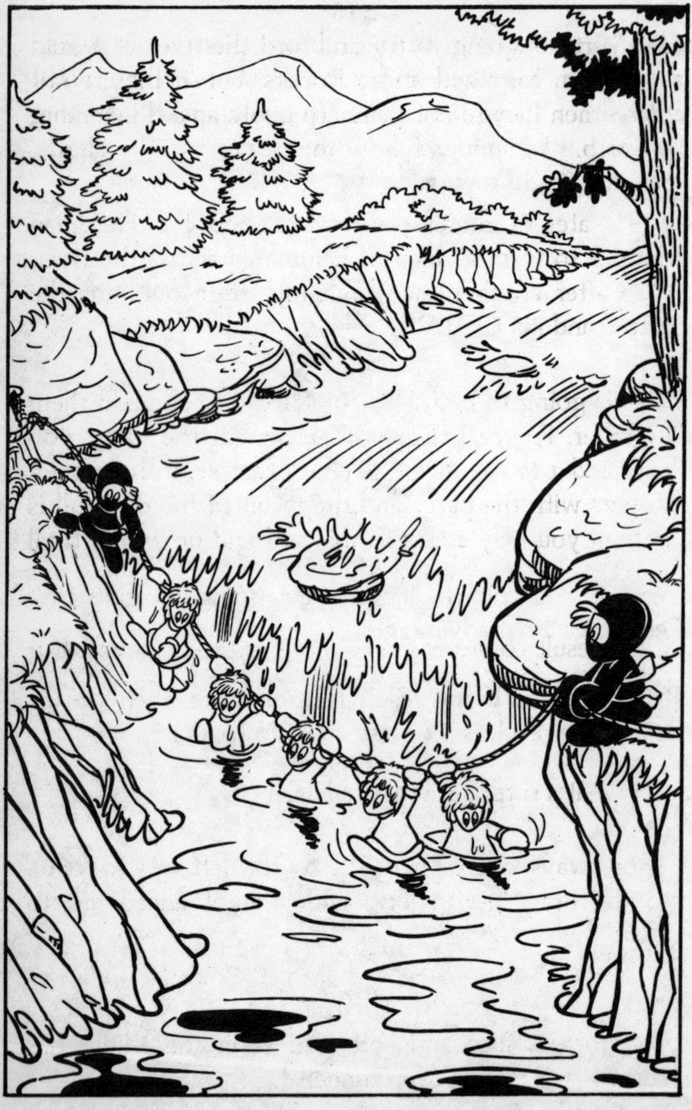

228

The party is going to try and ford the river. It would have been easy with more Ropers, but 'If they're not there, then they're not there!' to quote an old Lemming proverb.

The water is running very fast, and the Herdman decides to form a chain of Lemmings across the river. One after another the Lemmings edge out into the water, and it's COLD!

This is going to be tricky. Roll two dice and add them together. For each Roper that is with the party you may add 1 to the dice roll. (For example, if there are 3 Ropers with the party and the result of the dice roll is 6, then you may add 3 to this and end up with a total of 9.)

If the result comes to 10 or more, then go to **255**. If it is less than 10, go to **13**.

229

Oh what a surprise . . . more Maze!

Three ways out of here . . . to the left (go to **166**), to the right (go to **214**) and straight ahead (go to **186**).

230

The rock is nice and soft, and soon the Miner has constructed quite a deep tunnel.

Which way now? Will you carry on in the same direction (go to **160**) or turn a little to the left (go to **287**)?

231
The Lemmings are now marched off indoors. Where can they be going? Go to **327**.

232
Oops! Most of the Lemmings got across, but unfortunately one Flame Thrower didn't quite make it ... all that heavy equipment, you know. (If there wasn't a Flame Thrower in the party to start with, it looks like it's your lucky day!)

Now go to **318**.

233
Well, it took them a long time, but eventually the Builders make a bridge across the hole and the Lemmings march across.

Go to **284**.

234
Oh dear, there just aren't enough Ropers in the party to reach the top of the mast. Looks as if the Lemmings are going to have to think of something else (go to **199**).

235

Now the Lemmings find themselves trapped on a small section of the pier. There's no way they can make their way back to the end and get to the beach. It looks as if their only choice will be to try and get back to land and then look for another way. Unfortunately, that isn't going to be easy either.

The Lemmings must have a Builder in the party. If there isn't one, then the Lemmings have had it and will have to start again. Yes, you've guessed it . . .

Your adventure ends here!

If you have Builders, and if there is also an Attractor in the party, then go to **76**. If you don't have an Attractor, then go to **66**.

236

The Ropers take careful aim at the spaceship and then let fly. The ropes fly across and all of them hit the side of the ship and stick fast. As quickly as they can, the other Lemmings scrabble across to the spaceship and relative safety.

Now go to **394**.

237

The next two events are the long jump and the triple jump.

Which one do you think the Lemmings should try

first: the long jump (go to **49**) or the triple jump (go to **167**)?

238

The lake is frozen solid and is as smooth as glass.

Do you have any Skaters in the party? If you do, then go to **269**. If you don't, then you'll have to head for the snowfield (go to **156**).

239

If there are 5 or more Builders in the party, this presents no problems (go to **185**). If there are Builders in the party, but there are fewer than 5 of them, go to **256**.

If you have no Builders at all, then you *must* use the drawbridge (go to **264**).

240

The Attractor starts to do its stuff and, after a brief pause, the Skaters are off the ice and back in line.

Perhaps the Lemmings had better head for the snowfield now (go to **156**).

241

Well, it certainly pays to take risks sometimes! The Lemmings sail into the air, and the jump seems to go on for ever! (Make a note of the chance the Lemmings took!) Go to **273**.

242

The bulk of the Lemmings stop dead in their tracks, allowing the Builders to get to work. In no time at all a bridge is built.

Oops, looks like you're going to have to explode the Blocker so that the Lemmings can get across the bridge. Ah well, never mind, what a way to go!

Remove the Blocker from the party strength, and then go to **46**.

243

The rock is nice and soft, and soon the Miner has constructed quite a deep tunnel.

What now? Do you want him to carry on in the same direction (go to **105**) or turn a little to the right (go to **206**)?

244

That's it. Blast the asteroid out of the way! Not exactly subtle but — with a bit of luck — effective. Let's see, shall we? Go to **177**.

245

Oh NO! That Lemming just wasn't careful enough. With a trip, a Lemming of your choice goes tumbling into a crevasse . . . 'EUGHHH!!!'

Now the Lemmings may either go south (go to **328**) or head west (go to **56**).

246

As the Lemmings move deeper into the ice field, large gullies start to appear where the ice has melted, revealing the ocean underneath. In some places there are only isolated islands of ice to stand on.

The Lemmings cannot move any further east, the way's blocked by gullies.

Which way will they go now: south (go to **373**), east (go to **48**) or south-east (go to **196**)?

247

Roll one dice and add the result to the number of Spearers in the party. If you've been dumb enough not to include any Spearers, then you'll just have to make do with the dice.

Make a note of the total the Lemmings have scored, and then go to **208**.

248

This path soon opens into a small, gloomy clearing. Standing in the middle is the blackened remains of a giant oak tree.

Two paths lead from the clearing, one going south-westwards (go to **89**) and the other to the south-east (go to **108**).

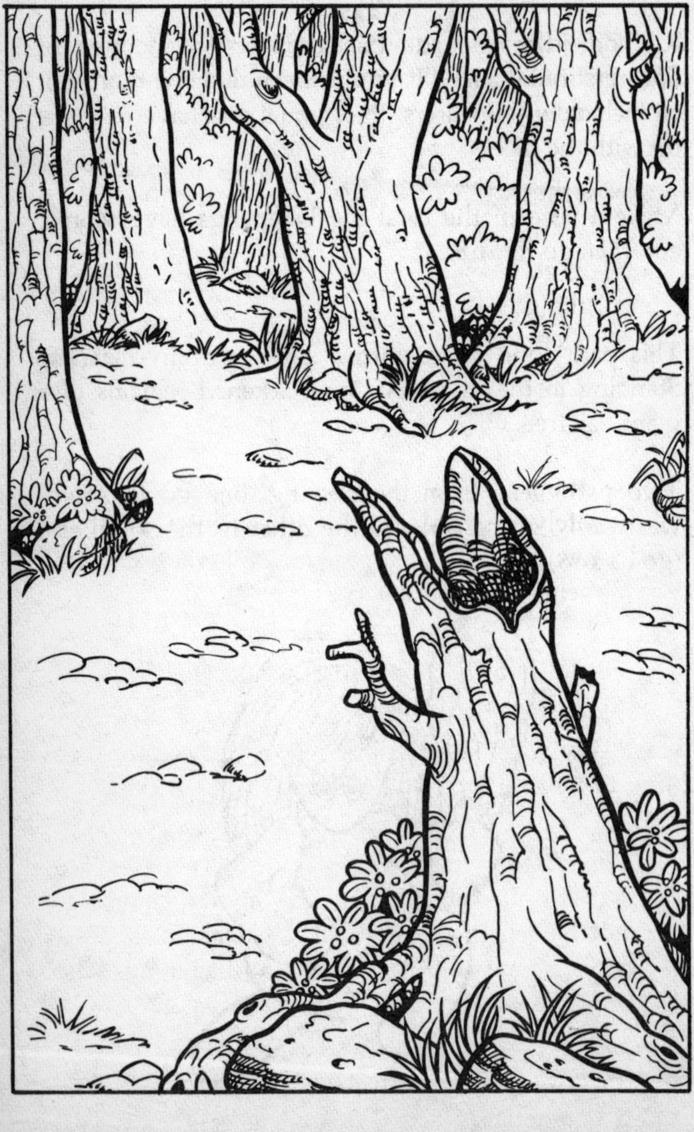

249

At last, a little bit of open space! The pathway opens into a sort of circular clearing, and there aren't quite so many shadows here.

It looks as though there are four ways to go now:

> Top left, go to **57**.
> Top right, go to **99**.
> Bottom left, go to **201**.
> Bottom right, go to **260**.

250

The Lemmings bravely set out into the ice field. Unfortunately, it's summer at the moment — not that you'd know it — but the weather is still warm enough to have melted some of the ice.

The ice field is now a very dangerous place.

Which way will the Lemmings go: to the west (go to **48**) or to the east (go to **225**)?

251

Unlike most other Lemmings, the Sports Lemmings have not hidden their part of the Medallion. Instead, they decide to award it to the party of Lemmings who win the Lemipics.

The games are just about to start. Go to **127**.

252

So it's going to be the Green Lever, is it ... Let's see what happens.

Go to **102**.

253

While the judges are working out the scores, you may compete in the javelin if the Lemmings have not already done so. Go to **121**.

If the Lemmings *have* already competed in the javelin or have been told that they cannot, then go to **169**.

254

Not wanting to be disqualified, the Lemmings decide to take off well before the start-line, though this means that the jump isn't going to be as long as it might have been. Go to **273**.

255

The last of the Lemmings struggles triumphantly out of the water and on to the far bank. Just on the other side of a hedge they can see the path that leads towards Castle Hollow . . . 'YIPPEE!'

Go to **210**.

256

You must now roll one dice and add the result to the number of Builders you have in the party. If the result is 7 or more, then the bridge has been built and you may go to **185**.

If the result is less than 7, then two Builders fall into the moat . . .

'SPLOSH!'

They get out OK, but now they are so smelly they are sent home immediately. Remove them from your party, then use the drawbridge (go to **264**).

257

The Blocker rushes to the head of the column and takes up his position. The Lemmings immediately start to turn back the way they have just come. Phew, that was a close shave.

Unfortunately, once a Blocker goes into Blocking Mode that's it, so you must remove this Lemming from your party (yes, do it now!).

You've avoided the pool and must now head for the stairs, so go to **203**.

258
Now that the Lemmings have decided on an angle, they must choose how far the cannon will shoot; they do this by adjusting a dial, which is labelled 'Bang ... Boom ... You Sure?' Make a note of the setting chosen and then go to **312**.

259
In the shadows the Lemmings can just make out three paths leading from this point. One leads to the left (go to **214**), one to the right (go to **26**), and the third leads more or less back the way they've just come (go to **77**).

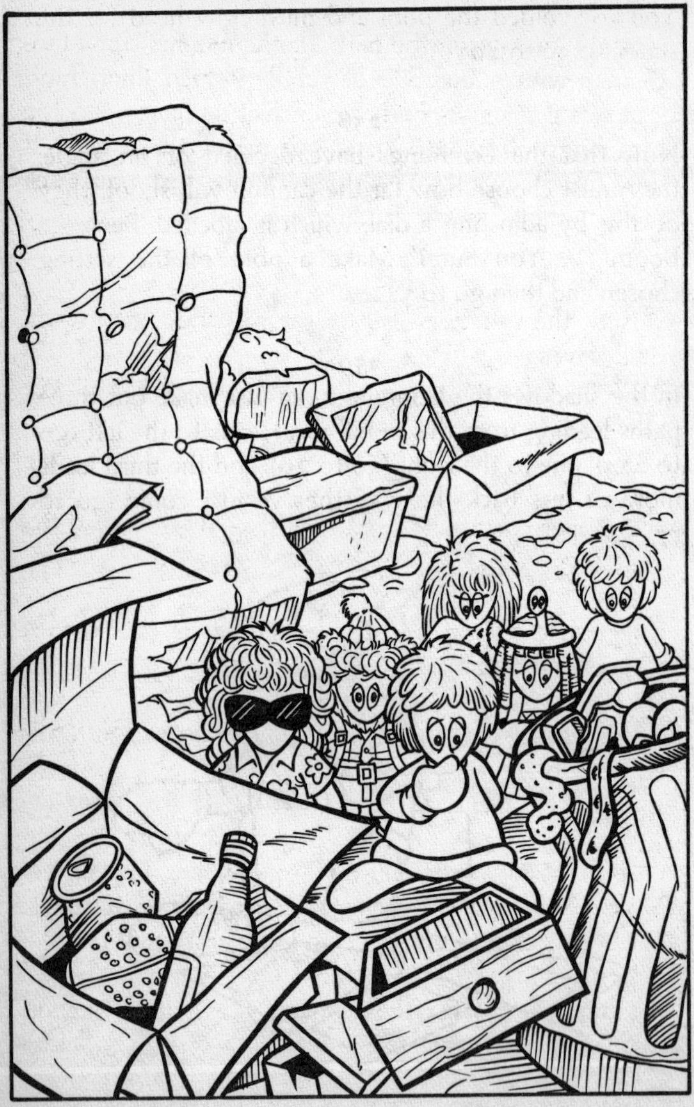

260

Turning a corner in the path, the Lemmings come face to face with a big pile of rubble, which (hint, hint) looks as if it might burn, given half a chance! Do the Lemmings want to try and get rid of the rubble? If they do, then go to **299**. Or will they just walk back the way they came (go to **201**)?

261

Wisely, the Lemmings set off for a gentle jog to warm themselves up.

Go to **67**.

262

The Roper takes careful aim and fires at the top of the mast.

Roll one dice and add the result to the number of Ropers in the party.

If the result is 9 or more, then go to **301**. If the result is 8 or less, then go to **234**.

263

Oops! This wasn't supposed to happen. The whole place is infested with crabs. Not particularly big ones, but big enough to give a Lemming a nasty nip!

Added to that, the tide is coming in – is there no end to a Lemming's problems?

The crabs are going to slow down the next task, which is to dig through to the central tower of the sandcastle. The Diggers have already set to work on this, but they are being hassled by the crabs.

Are there any Jumpers in the party? If there are, then go to **365**. If there aren't (sharp intake of breath!), go to **74**.

264
The Lemmings march briskly across the drawbridge, whistling as they go to cover the ominous creaking sounds — and in no time at all the Lemmings are on the other side. Go to **185**.

265
Suddenly there's no floor! Before the Lemmings can find out what's happened, one of them has fallen into an unseen pit. Remove one Lemming of your choice from the party, and then go to **30**.

266
Looks like it's going to be a swim — we hope you guessed right!

Roll one dice and add the result to the number of Swimmers that you chose. The Lemmings don't score anything for the Divers, but lose 2 points for any Pole Vaulters selected and 1 point for any other type of Lemming chosen.

Make a note of the final score and then go to **219**.

267

On closer inspection, the Lemmings discover a lever on the side of the cannon; it is labelled 'Low ... Med ... High'.

The Lemmings must decide at what angle to tilt the cannon; they can do this by adjusting the lever. Make a note of the setting you choose, and then go to **258**.

268

It certainly pays to take risks sometimes! The Lemmings sail into the air and the jump seems to go on for ever! (Make a note of the chance the Lemmings took!) Go to **273**.

269

The Skaters take one look at the ice and go into a frenzy! They just have to skate and, in no time at all, the lake is covered in twirling Skaters. It's quite a show — only the Skaters are enjoying themselves so much they seem to have forgotten all about the quest.

What are you going to do now? Is there an Attractor in the party? If there is, then go to **240**. If there isn't one, then you'll have to go to **8**.

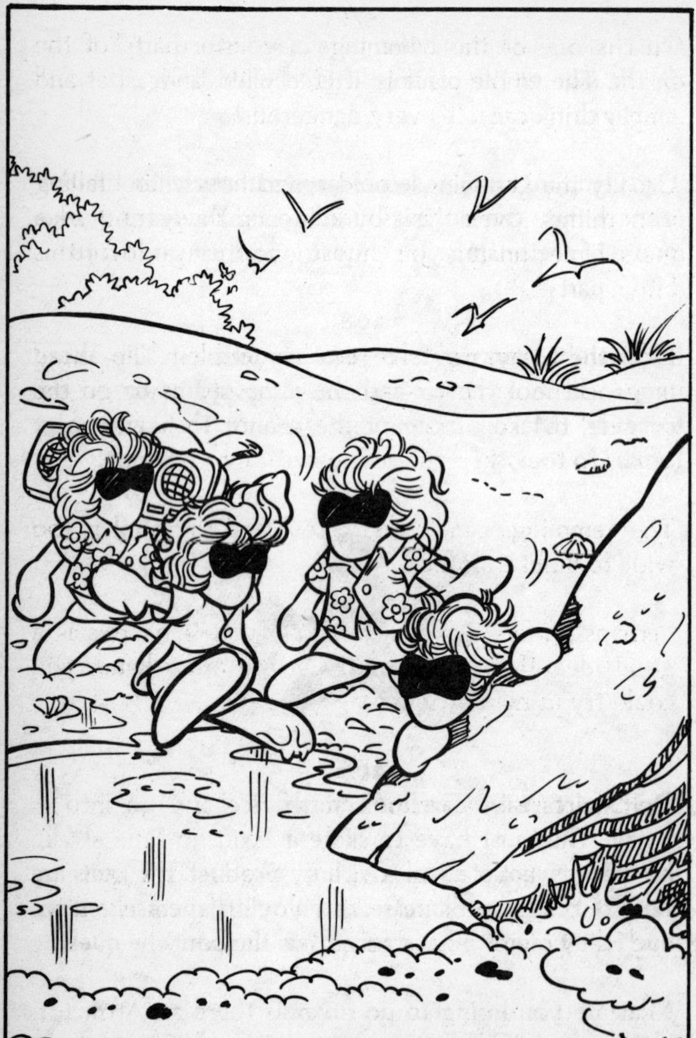

270

This is one of the Lemmings' favourite parts of the beach. The whole place is littered with sandcastles and empty drink cans. It's very dangerous!

Usually the Lemmings could spend hours here: falling into things, over things and generally getting in a mess. Unfortunately, it's onwards and upwards for this brave party!

Now the Lemmings have another problem. Up ahead is a rock pool. There's a bridge already made on the far side, but some Lemming is going to have to get across to the other side and lower it into position.

The Lemmings can't wade across and the pool is too wide to build a bridge.

Perhaps Surfers may be useful? If you think this is a good idea, then go to **195**. On the other hand, you could try using a Swimmer (go to **145**).

271

Duff staircase + Careless Lemmings = ?

'Oops,' is what it equals. As a by-product, the lions are not so hungry any more and you'll have to remove one Lemming of your choice from the party.

Once you've done this, go to **378**.

272

Oh NO! Just as the Lemmings almost reach the end of the pier, it finally gives up the ghost and starts to collapse under their poor feet. But by an utter fluke, all the Lemmings manage to scramble to safety.

Now go to **235**.

273

Now it's time to work out how well the Lemmings did in those last two events. For the triple jump, add up the number of Runners and Jumpers in the party and then roll one dice and add these numbers all together.

For the long jump, just add up the number of Jumpers in the party and then roll one dice, then add these two numbers together. Now, just to complicate matters (what, again!) if the Lemmings 'took a chance' in an event, then they may add 2 extra points to their score.

The Lemmings can now go to the medal ceremony (which might be a good idea, considering that the Lemmings need all the medals they can get!) in which case go to **278**. Alternatively, they can make for the final event (go to **44**).

274

The Stackers and Builders work as a perfect team, and in no time at all a broad staircase is built across the lion's cage. Go to **378**.

275

Which way will the Miners dig (just saying 'down' is not acceptable!)? If you reply: 'Straight down', go to **153**; 'Slightly over to the left', go to **243**; 'A little bit to the right', go to **230**.

276

The Laser Blasters blast away at the asteroid and huge chunks of it fly off in all directions. Sadly, some of these are still pretty big and they knock three Lemmings off the asteroid, never to be seen again. Remove them from the party, and then go to **329**.

277

POLE VAULTERS IN THE HIGH JUMP? YOU CHEAT!!!

The judges instantly disqualify the Sports Lemmings from the games – which of course means it's . . .

your-adventure-ends-here time!

278

To get a Gold Medal, the Lemmings need to have scored 12 points; to get a Silver, 10 points; and a Bronze, 8 points.

Make a note of any medals the Lemmings may have won, and then it's time for the next event, go to **44**.

279

Buzz, the head Lemming honcho, pushes the black button marked 'Eugh!' A large weight falls from the ceiling and squashes poor Buzz flatter than a pancake!

Don't despair! As we said, Buzz is the head Lemming and it takes more than being squashed flat to put a head Lemming out of the game. Unfortunately it'll take a while for him to recover.

Without the head Lemming, the other Lemmings are a shade depressed and confused. Until further notice, the Lemmings must reduce all their dice rolls by 1.

All that having been said, the Lemmings still need to get down to the planet. So what will they do now: pull the green lever marked, 'Yippee!' (go to **252**) or twist the red dial marked, 'Oops!' (go to **21**)?

280

The Jet Pack Lemming zooms up into the air (rather gracefully for a Lemming as a matter of fact!) and flies over to the spaceship — where the illusion is shattered as it hits the side of the ship with a thump!

Battered and bruised, go to **202**.

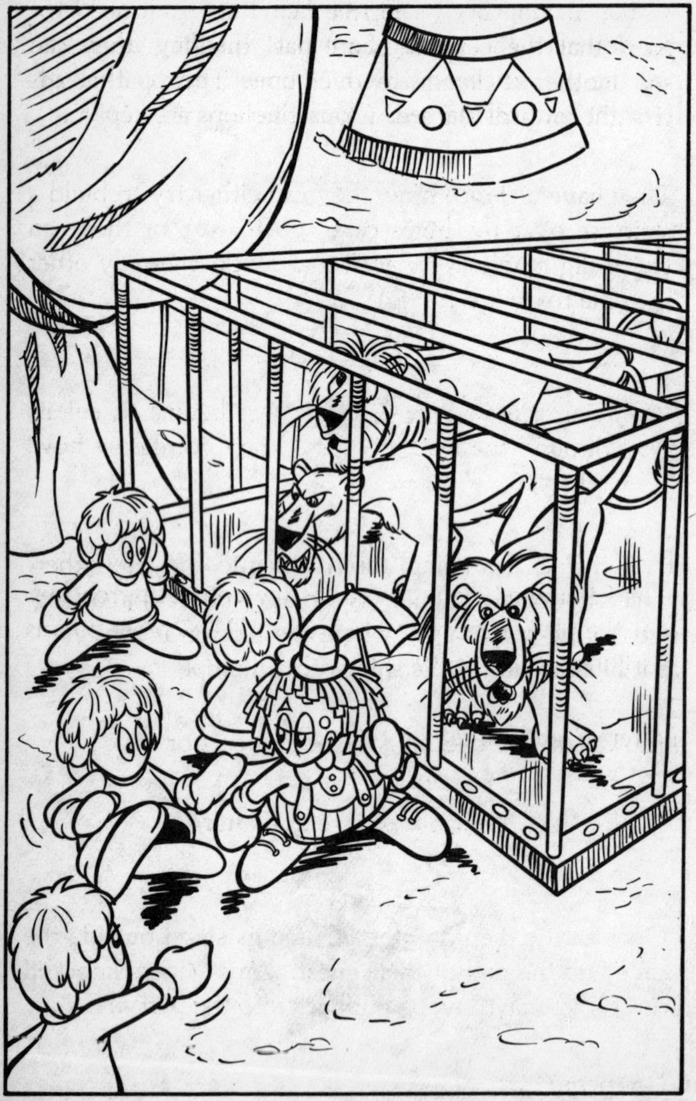

281

Now that the Lemmings are past the ring, they can see another challenge to overcome. Their path leads straight towards the area where the lions are kept.

They have a choice now: they can either try to build a staircase over the lion's cage (go to **96**), or they can try to dig a hole in the wall that blocks the only other possible route (go to **189**).

282

Whipping out its sword, the Fencer begins to cut its way through the wall; it's easy when you know how! ... Go to **378**.

283

The Lemmings wait, poised, as the comet approaches, but the platform is a little bit short. The comet zooms past, just out of reach!

Ah well, it'll be back in another 50 years or so . . .

Your adventure ends here.

284

Once across the pool, the Lemmings stand outside the cave and the end of their quest. (Any Miners knocked out earlier may now be put back into the party.)

Go to **170**.

285

At last the Miner breaks through and the Lemmings tumble on to the platform below.

Go to **81**.

286

After a short walk the Lemmings come to the edge of the ice field. To the east, there is only the open sea.

Where will they go now: west (go to **225**) or northwest (go to **246**)?

287

The tunnel is going like a dream.

Which way should they continue digging the tunnel? Should they carry on the same way (go to **396**), turn a little to the left (go to **344**) or turn sharply to the right (go to **14**)?

288

The Lemmings find themselves on a flat platform. To the left, a huge iron wall looms up into the clouds: you can't go that way. To the right, there is a large hill.

Go to **289**.

289

The hill is rather odd: there are huge arrows all over it and they seem to be pointing towards the Lemmings.

What should they do now? Should they try to bash their way through (there must be a Basher in the party to do this)? If you want them to do this, go to **352**. Alternatively, you could try sending a Climber up the hill to have a look around (go to **46**).

290

The penguins waddle over to meet the Lemmings, wagging their heads from side to side and falling over occasionally. They look very friendly and start to follow the Lemmings.

Will the Lemmings let the penguins tag along, or will they shoo them away?

Make a note of what the Lemmings decide to do, and then go either south (go to **56**) or south-west (go to **111**).

291

The mouth of the cave is pitch black, and there is a funny smell coming from it, too: it's sort of warm and a bit musty.

'zzzzZZZZ!'

Now, did you decide to bring those penguins along? You remember them, don't you, the ones from back on the icefield?

If you did, then go to **349**. If you didn't, then go to **368**.

292

The head Lemming of the Classic Zone, Plato Lemminus, leads the party to the edge of the trapdoor. The giant door swings open and it is time to go . . .

'Yippee!'

Go to 300.

293

The ground is growing rocky and uneven. Occasionally there is even the odd ray of sunshine. The trees are definitely getting further and further apart. Could it be that the Lemmings are at last reaching the edge of the forest?

Eventually they come to a T-junction.

Will they turn right (go to 375)? Or will they be tempted to go to the left (go to 40)?

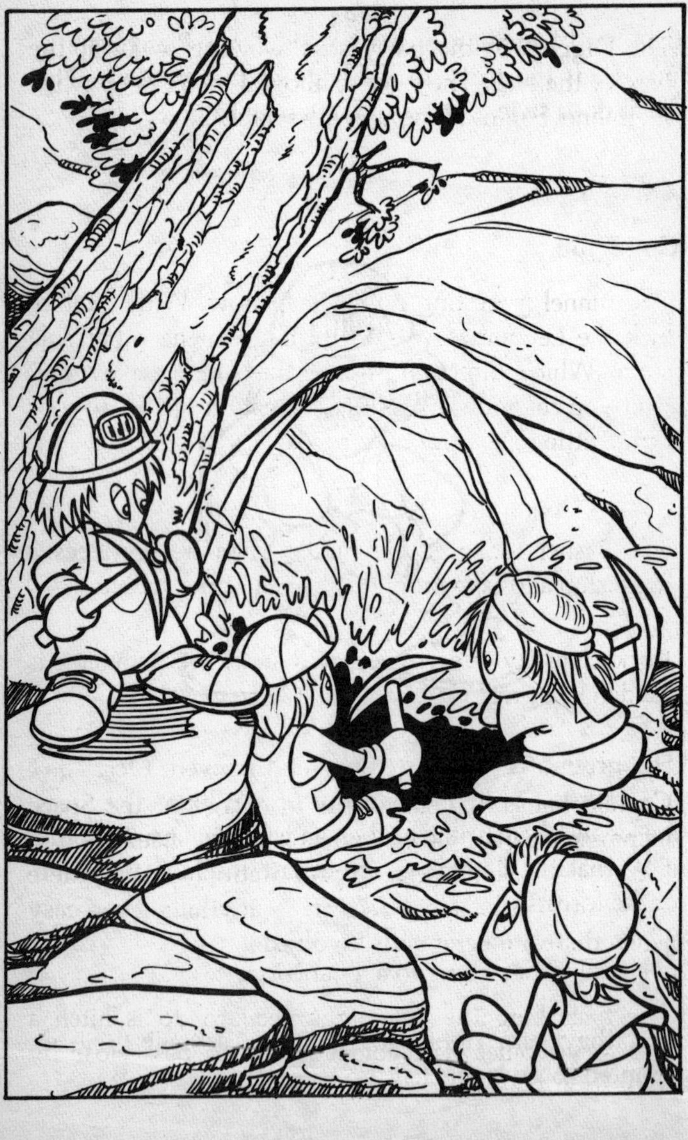

294

The Diggers in the party start working away at the base of the wall. They get to about a metre deep when the tunnel begins filling up with water.

Go to **9**.

295

The tunnel is getting rather deep now. With a bit of luck the Lemmings will be through to the other side soon. Which direction should the tunnel take now? Will you carry on in the same direction (go to **105**) or turn a little to the right (go to **305**)?

296

The Basher looks at the rubble, then he produces a huge club and takes a mighty swing at the rubble.

Rock chips fly everywhere, and soon the Lemming is hidden in a great cloud of dust. Go to **2**.

297

Captain James T. Lemming is in charge of the Space Lemmings party. James knows that the Medallion is hidden in an old, deserted Space Station. Getting there is no easy task – let's face it, is anything ever easy when there are Lemmings involved!)

The first thing the Lemmings need to do is hitch a ride on a comet. The comet is due to pass close by very soon.

How will the Lemmings reach it? Will they use a Platformer (go to **316**) or a Roper (go to **354**)?

298

This is a job for ... SUPER LEM! (Fanfare of trumpets etc.)

Super Lem! flies straight at the asteroid and smashes it out of the way!

The other Lemmings are safe but the Super Lem! has used up all its power and now floats away helplessly. Ahhh, never mind! Remove the Super Lem! from the party strength and remember its deeds with pride.

Now go to **329**.

299

A Flame Thrower will be able to get rid of the rubble easily. Unfortunately, each Flame Thrower can be used only once. If the Flame Thrower is used, you may remove the rubble and then go to **363**.

If you decide to do this, make a note that one Flame Thrower is now 'out of fuel'. You'd best be careful here since there's no guarantee that the rubble won't be back again if the Lemmings retrace their steps!

If you prefer the Lemmings to retrace their steps and try another path, then go to **201**.

300

The Lemmings drop in a neat row on to the platform below. When the last has landed – and very elegantly this was too, none of your landing on another Lemming's head with a squelch – it's make-your-mind-up time.

Will the Lemmings go left towards a pool of water (go to **346**) or will they go right towards some stairs (go to **203**)?

301

The Roper just manages to get a rope up to the top of the mast so that the Lemmings can climb up it.

Go to **324**.

302

The paths soon ends at a T-junction. Obviously, there's no point in going back the way they have just come (even the Lemmings have figured that out for themselves!) So, what's it going to be, the path going left (go to **322**) or the one going right (go to **214**)?

303

Now the Lemmings are led back into the building where the swimming pool is.

Choose your Lemmings and then go to **361**.

304

It's very dangerous to start this sort of thing without warming up the poor old Lemmings.

Roll one dice. If the score is 4 or more, then go to **171**. If it's 3 or less, then go to **197**.

305

This is getting good: the tunnel is progressing well, with no problems.

Which way will the tunnel go now? Do you want to carry on in the same direction (go to **68**), turn a little to the left (go to **115**) or turn sharply to the left (go to **105**)?

306

The Medieval Lemmings have succeeded! Their part of the Great Medallion has been found. Make a note of this joyous fact. Now go to **20**, and continue the quest!

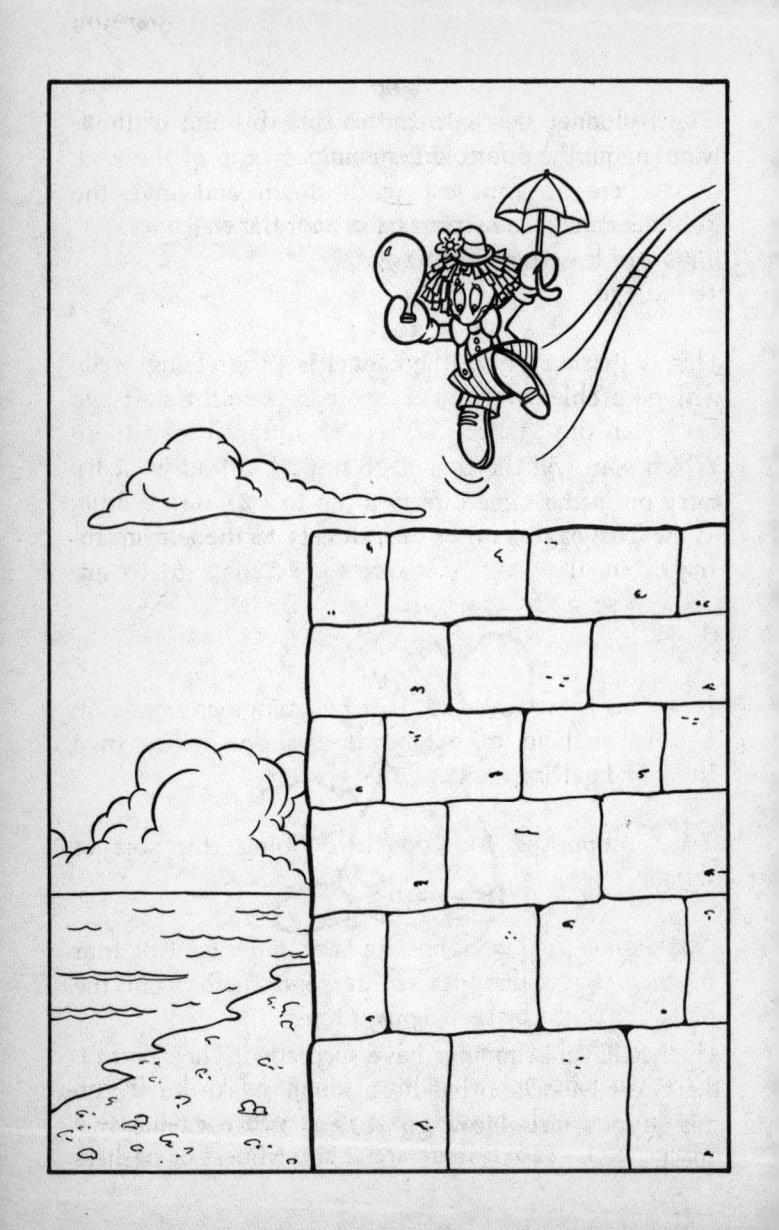

307

The Ballooner sails into the air and, by one of those strange quirks of fate, drifts neatly on top of the wall. From here he can just reach down and give the other Lemmings a helping hand over the wall.

Go to **270**.

308

Oh NO! The Lemmings have stepped on the start-line and been disqualified! Still ... if you will take these chances ...

If they haven't already competed in, or been disqualified from, the long jump, then they may go to **49**. Otherwise, go to **273**.

309

Now this is just the stuff that Lemmings are made of! Dozens of them are milling around, doing their own thing and getting exactly nowhere.

You're supposed to stop them doing this sort of thing!!!

By the time the Lemmings are back under control, four of them have disappeared (remove them from the party), never to be seen again. Oops!

Now what do you want the Lemmings to do? If you want to use a Basher, go to **296**. If you want to use a Miner, go to **226**. If there aren't any Miners or Bashers left in the party, then the Lemmings (and you) have blown it, it's back to square one!

Your adventure ends here!

310

The path leads away from the town and into the forest. It is a lovely sunny day – in fact a perfect day for a picnic.

This part of the forest, near the town, is well known to our Lemmings: it is an ideal place for strolls and picnics. Unfortunately, the Lemmings are going to have to walk a lot further than that!

After about half an hour, the Lemmings come to the top of a hill. Looking down, they can see a river with a small bridge crossing it. Go to **362**.

311

To become overall champions, the Sports Lemmings need to have got more medal points than any one else. To work out medal points, look at all the medals the Sports Lemmings have won. Score 3 points for each Gold Medal, 2 points for each Silver Medal and 1 point for each Bronze Medal.

If the Sports Lemmings have scored 10 medal points or more, then go to **64**. If they have scored 9 or less, then go to **109**.

312

A brave Lemming has already climbed into the cannon and is waiting expectantly.

Now let's see what happens next. Go to **192**.

313

Roll one dice. If the result is 3 or more, then go to **104**. If the result is 2 or less, then go to **333**.

314

The Lemmings set off in the opposite direction, but after only a few moments they come to the edge of the platform. It just stops short, opening into a (probably) bottomless pit. They're going to have to go back and walk towards those points of light. Go to **355**.

315

A small path leads downstream. After a short while the Lemmings come to a part of the stream that looks shallower than usual.

If the Lemmings have at least 4 Ropers in the party, then go to **255**. If they have fewer than 4 Ropers in the party, then go to **228**.

316

This seems like a good idea. The Platformers get to work and soon there is a long platform leading out towards the comet.

Even so, it's still not going to be easy ... Go to **350**.

317
Now the Lemmings have come to a crossroads. There's probably no point in retracing their steps, so they have a choice of three ways to go: straight on (go to **93**), off to the left (go to **143**) or off to the right (go to **77**).

318
There are two more pits in front of the Lemmings. However, with a little squeezing, they should just be able to get round them. Go to **381**.

319
The track now comes to a crossroads – so much choice!

North: go to **139**.
South: go to **293**.
East: go to **375**.
West: go to **108**.

320
Welcome to the Classic Zone. This is where it all started, and this Zone, so it is said, is where the Lemmings started off in life.

The Classic Zone is a weird and wonderful place, full of pillars and metal floors, odd little holes and bubbling lakes. It was here that the Lemmings first acquired their taste for danger and learnt how to do whatever they do.

This is the start of the Classic Zone. Before you go any further, you must select the Lemmings that will go on this part of the quest. How many you can have depends on the number of Lemmings you finished the last zone with. Simply trade in the Lemmings you already have for the new ones listed below on a one-for-one basis. If this is the first zone you have visited, then you may choose 50 Lemmings.

Lemmings available in the Classic Zone
Ballooner	Filler	Blocker
Stomper	Miner	Builder
Basher	Exploder	Climber

Once you have done this, make a note of the ones you have chosen, then go to **292**.

321

Roll one dice and add the score to the number of Skiers in the party. If the result is 7 or more, then go to **220**. If the result is less than 7, then go to **125**.

322

So, which way is it going to be now? You can either head off to the left (go to **357**) or turn right (go to **163**).

323

Inside the cave, the Lemmings blunder around for a while. All of a sudden, one yells out:

'YIPPEE, YIPPEE!'

The Lemmings have found a piece of the Great Medallion.

Make a note of this fact, then go to **20**.

324

It's a long old climb, but at last the Lemmings reach the top of the mast.

Now go to **161**.

325

OK then! The Rollers curl up into a ball and start to tumble down the slope. Let's see what happens, shall we? Go to **147**.

326

Well, that's it, then. No Laser Blaster, no comment, as they say ...

Your adventure ends here

327

The Lemmings find themselves on the side of a swimming pool. So what's it going to be: a dive or a swim? No one seems to know. Choose your Lemmings now and then go to **266**.

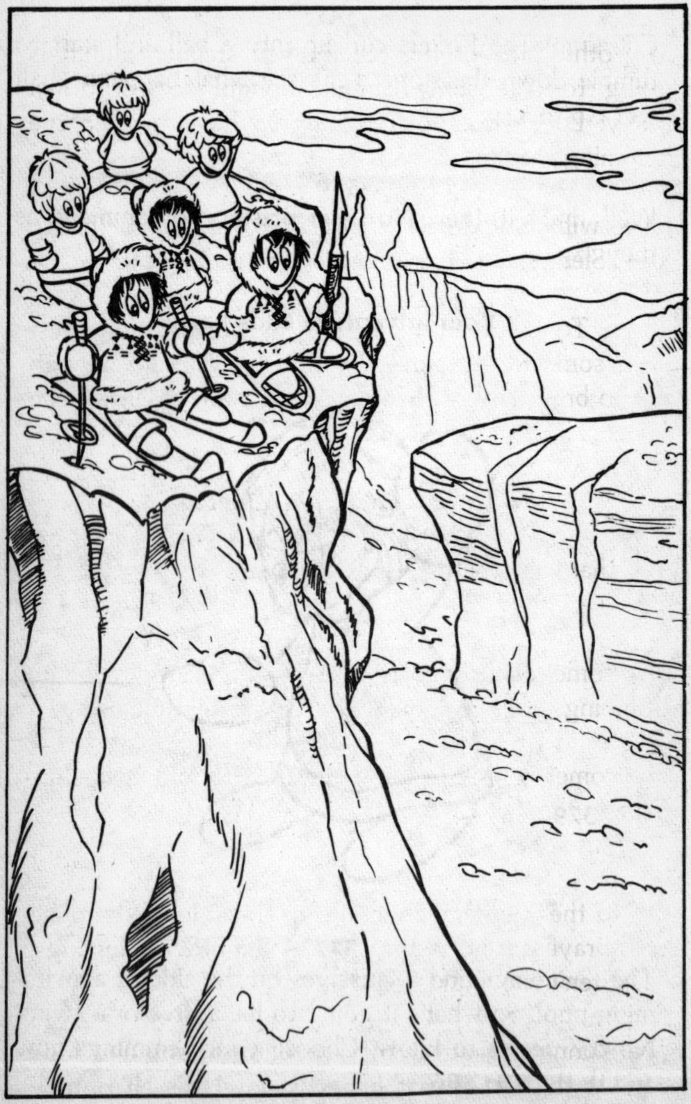

328

The other side of the hill is even steeper, and it is going to take some careful thought to get down safely. Looks like you're going to have to help the Lemmings again.

How will they do it? They could use Skiers (go to 391), Sledgers (go to 90) or Rollers (go to 325).

NOTE: To use Skiers, Sledgers or Rollers, you must have some in the party. If you've been silly enough not to bring any of them in the party, then all we can say is . . .

Your adventure ends here.

Yes, that was what we said! Bye, bye.

329

The comet is through the asteroid field now and the Lemmings are safe again — at least for the time being.

The comet is now heading towards the old spaceship. Go to 379.

330

Off to the Runners, zooming up the side of the dune and spraying sand in the faces of the other Lemmings, who aren't too impressed!

The Runners stand at the top of the dune and look back at the rest. What happens now? It's all right —

you don't have to answer that, we'll tell you. Nothing is what happens. The Runners get bored after a while and come back to the rest of the party. You're going to have to try something else. Go back to **218**.

331

The path runs through a steep gorge now, and it's impossible for even the most sharp-eyed of Lemmings to see more than a few centimetres in front of his face.

Suddenly the Herdman Lemming raises a hand. A signal to stop!

Up ahead, the path has been blocked by a rockfall. The Herdman runs an expert hand over the fallen rocks and sinks into deep thought.

The Lemmings have a choice here. Should they try and dig through the rockfall (the Lemmings must have at least one Basher and one Miner in the party to attempt this)? If so, go to **347**. If you think it would be safer all round to walk back and follow the path to the woods, then go to **310**.

332

Two paths lead away at this Y-junction. One, straight ahead, disappears in the distance — which isn't very far in this light (go to **107**). The other curves slowly away to the left (go to **392**).

333

On balance (or perhaps the lack of it) trying to get across on the tightrope wasn't such a good idea. Two poor Lemmings tumble to the ground in the crossing and land with a mighty thump! All they'll be doing for the rest of the adventure is looking at the shooting stars spinning round their heads! Remove two Lemmings of your choice from the party and then go to **281**.

334

The normally sleepy village of Lemhaven is a hive of activity. Everywhere Lems are rushing this way and that.

In the village square a group of Lemmings is waiting for the village Herdman to arrive. The time has come for the Medallion to be made whole again, and to find the medieval fragment which was buried deep in the dungeons of Castle Hollow, the long-deserted palace of the Old Kings that lay on the far side of the forest.

Getting it back is going to be no easy thing, and the village's finest have assembled to attempt the task. Suddenly a hush falls over the Lemmings and each one snaps to attention. The Herdman has arrived, a Lemming of above-average height and heavy build. On his head he proudly wears the scarlet beret worn by all village leaders.

For a few seconds he gazes at the ranks of Lems, then he utters a single phrase ... 'LETS GO!'

But which way will the Lemmings go?
   Towards the hills, go to **370**.
   Towards the woods, go to **310**.

335

Over in a corner of the tent is the cannon used in the 'Human Cannonball' act. No reason at all why it can't be used for a 'Lemming Cannonball' act as well!

With a little luck the cannon should be able to fire the Lemming straight up on to the platform where the Medallion is; all they have to do is get the angle right. Go to **267**.

336

This is the start of the Medieval Zone. Before you go any further, you must select the Lemmings that will go on this part of the quest. How many you can have depends on the number of Lemmings you finished the last zone with. Simply trade in the Lemmings you already have for the new ones listed below on a one-for-one basis. If this is the first zone you have visited, then you may choose 50 Lemmings.

Lemmings available in the Medieval Zone

Jumper	Runner	Archer
Musician	Builder	Thrower
Basher	Miner	Roper

Once you have done this, make a note of the ones you have chosen, then go to **334**.

337

Unfortunately, someone has built a wall across this stretch of the beach. You know the sort, the kind that are supposed to stop the sand getting washed away.

Guess what, it's blocking the way. It's not all that high, just high enough to stop the Lemmings getting over it easily.

What will the Lemmings do? Should they try to build a tunnel underneath it using a Digger (go to **294**)? Perhaps they could use a Ballooner to get on top of the wall to help the others up (go to **307**).

338
The Laser Blasters are good shots! The asteroid disintegrates into thousands of tiny pieces and the Lemmings' comet sails through safely.

Well done! Go to **329**.

339
Roll one dice and add the result to the number of Jumpers you chose for this game. No other Lemmings count. However, if you chose any Pole Vaulters, then go to **277**.

Otherwise, make a note of the final score, and then go to **303**.

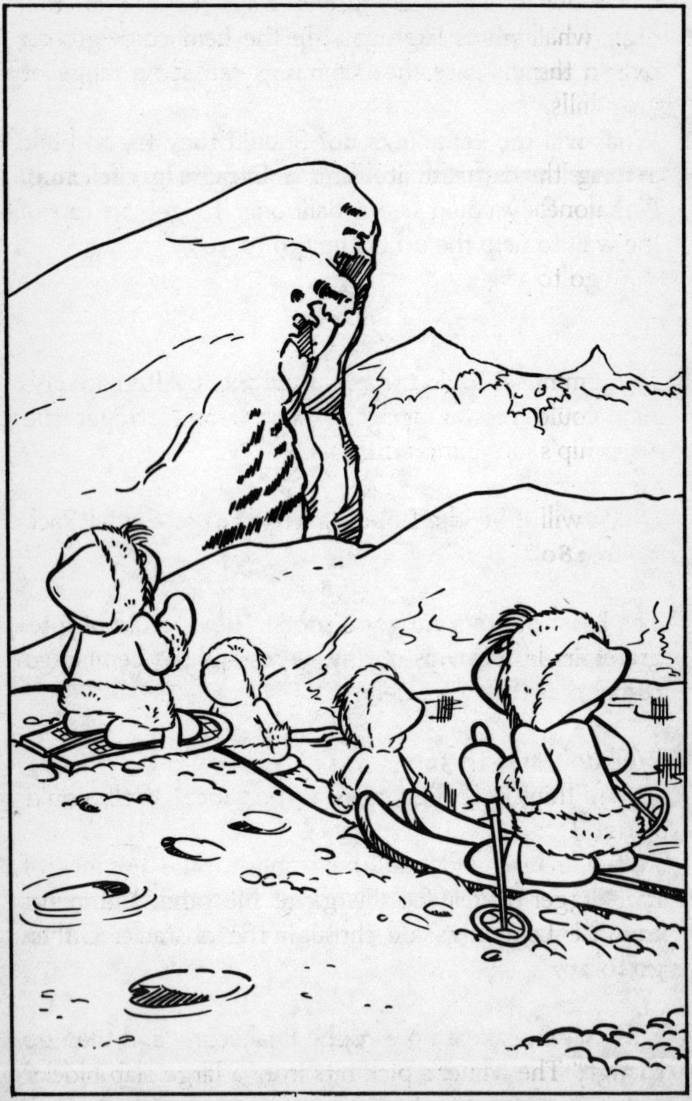

340

After what seems like ages, the ice field comes to an end. In the distance the Lemmings can see a range of steep hills.

Getting through the ice field was quite a challenge. Well done!

Now go to **384**.

341

The Lemmings could try and use Ropers. Alternatively, they could send a Jet Pack across and trigger the spaceship's grappling arm.

Which will it be, the Roper (go to **159**) or the Jet Pack (go to **280**)?

342

The stairs lead down to a small passageway ... Go to **369**.

343

So you think that digging is a good idea? Well, you'd be right!

The Digger makes short work of the sand, and in no time the Lemmings are through the obstacle. Go to **385**.

344

'Clang!!!' The Miner's pick hits iron: a large slab blocks

the tunnel. There's no getting through this way. Worse than that, the Miner's pick has broken and may not be used again.

This Lemming is not removed from the party strength, but may not be used again until we tell you. If this leaves you with no Miners ... Oops!

Your adventure ends here

Of course, if you've got lots of them, you can go to **243** and have another go.

345

At last the Lemmings pick their way through the rubble and find themselves in a large cavern. 'Let's go!' the Herdman exclaims and points to the far wall. Hanging on the wall is an odd-shaped, golden plate. It's part of the Medallion!

Unfortunately, there's a small fly in the ointment! Sitting immediately in front of the Medallion is a *large*, no, a VERY LARGE Dragon.

346–347

The Lemmings are going to have to deal with the Dragon before they can get to the Medallion.

If there is a Musician in the party, go to **17**.

Without a Musician, the Lemmings will have to attack the Dragon. Oh dear! Go to **366**.

346

Off march the Lemmings, with Plato at their head, straight towards the pool of water. Are you sure this is what you want?

Go to **200**.

347

The two Lemmings step bravely up to the rockfall and set to work.

After a few minutes' hard work, the face begins to move! Go to **398**.

348

None of the Lemmings can see yet. Each is holding on to the hand of the one in front so that the party can keep together.

Go to either **353** or **187**.

349

The penguins start to twitch their beaks and then charge — if a penguin can be said to 'charge', that is. Actually, it's more of a sort of waddle really.

A few seconds later a dreadful racket comes from inside the cave and suddenly a huge polar bear comes rushing out, hotly pursued by the penguins.

Hmmm, how strange! Still, at least the Lemmings can enter the cave in safety now.

Go to **323**.

350

Roll one dice and add the result to the number of Platformers in the party.

If the total is 8 or more, then go to **158**. If the total is 7 or less, then go to **283**.

351

Now the Lemmings have reached the spaceship, it's time to explore. Go to **394**.

352

On the face of it, this looks fairly easy but, try as it may, the Basher can't make a dent in the hill.

After ten minutes, Plato calls it a day. The Lemmings are going to have to try something else.

If there's a Climber in the party, then go to **205**.

If there aren't any Climbers, then it looks like that's it . . .

Your adventure ends here!

353

Suddenly there's no floor! Before the Lemmings realize what is going on, two of them have fallen into an unseen pit. Remove two Lemmings of your choice from the party, and then go to **187**.

354

This is not going to be easy. The comet will be moving very fast and will not be an easy target. Go to 3.

355

As the Lemmings get closer, the points of light begin to flash a little more quickly – what can they be?

It's only when the poor Lemmings are almost standing next to them that they realize . . . oops!

Go to 371.

356

This is getting good: the tunnel is progressing well with no problems.

Which way now, though? Will you carry on in the same direction (go to 68) or turn a little to the right (go to 122)?

357

Ah . . . more maze!

Go to **36**.

358

Nothing wrong with thinking about things — well, not as a rule. Unfortunately, while you are thinking about what to do, the tide comes in and swamps all the Lemmings.

Your adventure ends here.

Not a particularly impressive performance, was it?

359

A tangle of metal girders fills the corridor. Is there a Laser Blaster in the party?

If there is, then go to **380**. If there isn't, then go to **326**.

360

'Let's go!' the Herdman yells, and points at the rubble. Immediately, the whole party attacks the rubble in whatever way they can. It's an absolute shambles! Go to **309**.

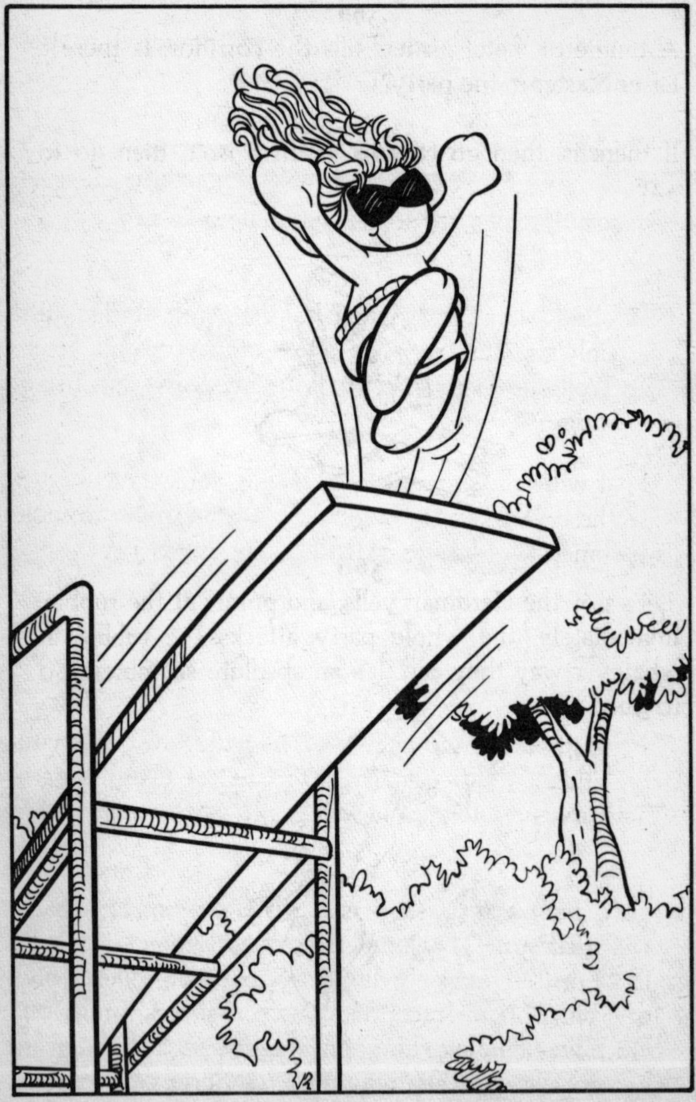

361

It's a dive! Roll one dice and add the result to the number of Divers in the party.

Deduct 1 point for each Spearer in the group.

Make a note of your score, and then go to **123**.

362

The bridge in the distance is the Troll Bridge. It's certainly the quickest way across the river – but then, the Troll may well object to so many Lemmings using his bridge!

What will the Lemmings do? If you think they should use the bridge, go to **221**. If they would prefer to look for some other way to cross the river, go to **315**.

363

And it's a ... Go to **116**.

364

Hmm, just a choice of two paths to follow here: you can either go straight on (go to **302**) or take the path that curves round a bit (go to **214**).

365

Now, *that* was a good idea. Lateral thinking, that's what *that* was! The Jumpers start to jump ... up and down on the crabs – who, of course, don't like it one little bit. This distracts them from their main mission, which was nipping the poor Diggers, so that they can now get on with their digging. Well done. Go to **100**.

366

Look at the party: score 1 point for each Archer, $\frac{1}{2}$ point for each Basher, and $\frac{1}{4}$ point for every other Lemming.

Add them all together then round fractions down (for example, $6\frac{3}{4}$ would become 6).

Now roll one dice and add the result to the number you have just worked out.

If the result is 12 or more, then the Lemmings have defeated the Dragon and may go to **306**.

If the result is less than 12, the Dragon has unfortunately eaten one Lemming! Remove one of your choice from the party, then attack the Dragon again.

Now the Lemmings have started, they must keep on trying until they have defeated the Dragon (go to **306**) or all the Lemmings have been eaten. In which case, of course . . .

Your adventure ends here!

367

Roll one dice. If the result is 3 or more, then go to **38**. If the result is 2 or less, then go to **388**.

368

Led by the brave Captain, the Lemmings march blindly into the cave. The 'zzzZZZ' noise gets gradually louder until it sounds more like 'GRRRRRRRR!'

Oh no, a polar bear must have been using the cave as a den! The Lemmings have stumbled in and woken it up. The Lemmings have no choice but to fight the bear.

Add up the number of Throwers in your party and score 1 point for each.

Now do the same for Attractors, and score $\frac{1}{2}$ a point for each of these. Score $\frac{1}{4}$ point for all the other Lemmings. Then add up all these points and round the result down (for example, a final score of $7\frac{1}{2}$ would count as 7).

Now roll one dice and add the result to your score. If the total is 12 or more, then the bear is beaten off and runs away (go to **323**).

If the score is less than 12, then the bear has beaten off the Lemmings. Sadly, some of the Lemmings may have been eaten as well!

Roll one dice. If the result is 4 or more, then the Lemmings can attack the bear again. If the result is 3 or less, then another Lemming has been eaten. Remove one Lemming of your choice from the party (remembering to adjust your score) then attack the bear again.

There's no going back now. The Lemmings must either defeat the bear or be eaten in the process.

Obviously, if all your Lemmings get eaten then it's ...

Your adventure ends here ...

'Buurrp' (Sorry, that was the bear!)

369
Now this is a bit strange: for the first time, the Lemmings can see a glimmer of light. Will they walk towards the light (go to **150**) or away from it (go to **106**)?

370
The path leads away from the town and up into the foothills of the Great Mountains. The path winds its way ever upwards, and soon the herd of Lemmings is surrounded by an eerie mist. Go to **331**.

371

Suddenly the points of light turn into *eyes*! The Lemmings have walked straight into a Shadow Monster ... argh!

With nowhere to run to, the Lemmings are going to have to fight. It's either that or let the monster eat them all (there's no paragraph you can go to for this!).

Go to **165**.

372

It's very dangerous to start strenuous exercise without warming up the poor old Lemmings first.

Roll one dice. If the score is 4 or more, then go to **247**. If it's 3 or less, then go to **209**.

373

This is the edge of the ice field. To the west, a vast range of mountains towers out of the ice. There is no chance that the Lemmings can go that way.

Which way should they go now: north-east (go to **250**) or east (go to **225**)?

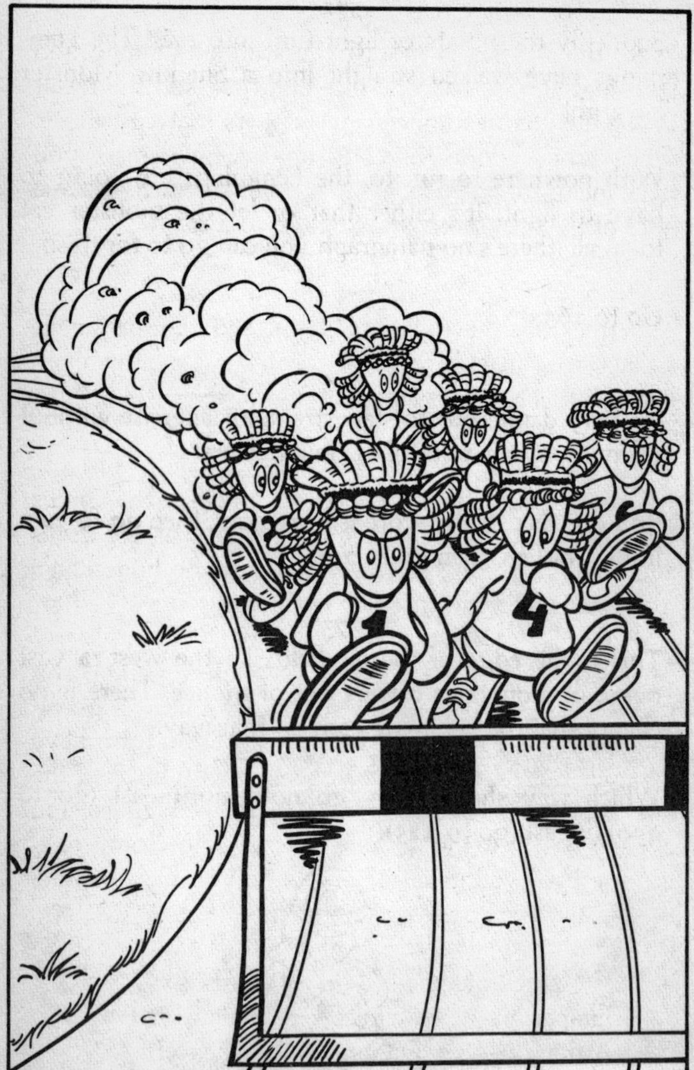

374

Well, the hurdles is more or less about running and then jumping, so roll one dice and then add the result to the number of Runners and Jumpers that you chose. Once you've done this, add up any Swimmers you have included, and take away 1 point for each. Make a note of the final score, and then go to **231**.

375

The trees are much thinner here, and the air smells fresher too. In the distance the Lemmings can even hear a bird singing. Now go to **390**.

376

Welcome to the Circus Zone: this is where the Circus Lemmings live. These little guys just love all the thrills and spills of the big top — though, to be honest, it's more spills than thrills!

This is the start of the Circus Zone: Before you go any further, you must select the Lemmings that will go on this part of the quest. How many you can have depends on the number of Lemmings you finished the last zone with. Simply trade in the Lemmings you already have for the new ones listed below on a one-for-one basis. If this is the first zone you have visited, then you may choose 50 Lemmings.

Lemmings available in the Circus Zone

Jumper	Builder	Stacker
Attractor	Digger	Fencer
Icarus Wings	Glue Pourer	SuperLem!

Once you have done this, make a note of the ones you have chosen, then go to **42**.

377

Without a Blocker, the poor Builders were never going to get the bridge built in time . . .

Go to **191**.

378

Now the Lemmings are past the lion, they're within sight of their goal. Unfortunately, the Medallion is perched high up in the canopy of the Big Top and there's no obvious way up.

Then the Lemmings spot just the thing! Go to **335**.

379

The ancient hulk of the spaceship looms up in front of the Lemmings. The spaceship will get the Lemmings down to the planet's surface where the Medallion is hidden. First, though, they've got to find some way to get off the comet and into the spaceship.

Hmmm, interesting problem. Think about it and go to **341**.

380

The Laser Blaster cuts through the girders in no time at all.

Now go to **120**.

381

YES! ... Guess you could say they passed the 'Outline Test'. (This is an old joke, so please accept our apologies. We remember the ZX 81, the Vic 20, Space Invaders — now that was a game! etc., etc. Yawn ... Yawn.) Sorry about that, don't know what came over us.

Now it's time to go to **128**.

382

So how well have the Lemmings done in this event? To get a Gold Medal, they will need to have scored at least 100 points; to get a Silver, 90 points; and to get a Bronze, 75 points.

Now go to 33.

383

After a short and uneventful walk, the Lemmings notice two small points of light in the distance; they are blinking on and off from time to time. How strange!

Will the Lemmings walk towards the points of light (go to 355) or will they walk away from them (go to 314)?

384

The hillside is covered in deep snow, and many of the Lemmings sink up to their waists as they plod up the slope.

By the time they reach the top, the Lemmings are more than a little tired!

Go to 328.

385

Welcome to the beach! This is a wonderful place. Sun, sea and sand, lots of sand!

Barbaranne looks around for a while and then points. 'This way. Let's go!'

Now go to 337.

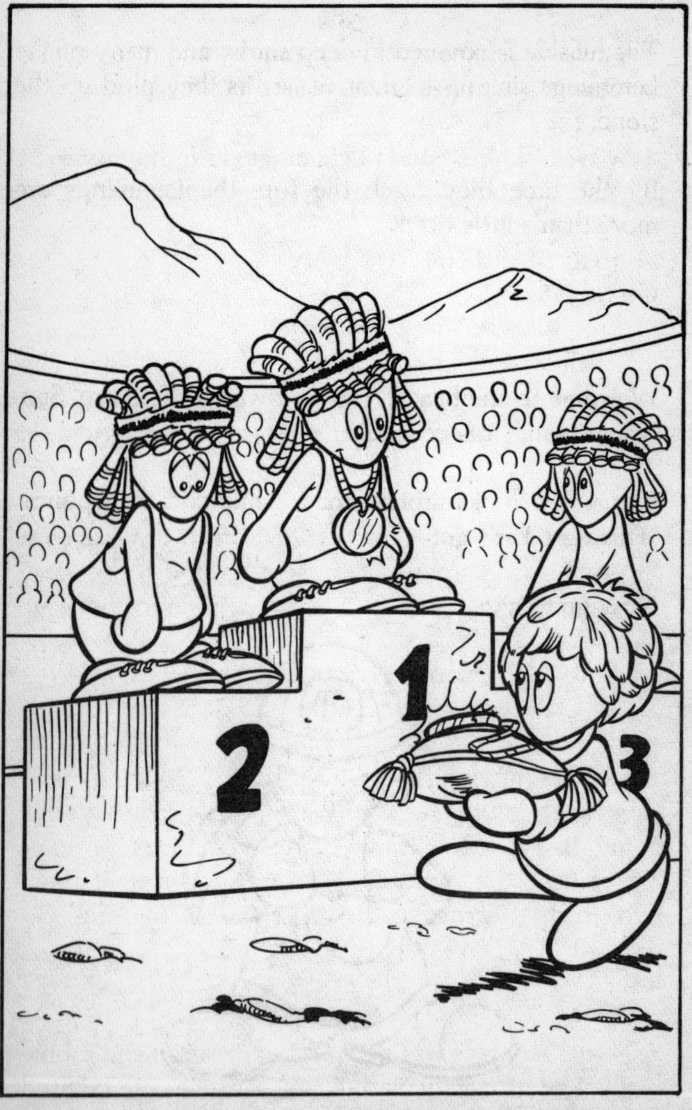
2
1
3

386

The awards ceremony is very grand — and it looks like the Sports Lemmings have got into the medals.

How well did the Sports Lemmings do in the first two events?

Go to **47** to find out.

387

The valley lies on the far side of a small hill. The castle here was once the palace of the king, but it has long since been abandoned — some even say it is haunted!

One thing's for sure: getting down into the dungeon and capturing the Medallion is not going to be easy. The ruins of the castle gradually come into view, its crumbling walls towering into the sky. This really is going to be a challenge! Go to **152**.

388

There's no dragging away three of the Lemmings who have been captivated by the clowns: sadly, you're going to have to remove three Lemmings of your choice from the party. Still, at least the rest of them have made it across to the other side of the ring. Go to **281**.

389

A Flame Thrower will be able to get rid of the rubble easily. Unfortunately, each Flame Thrower can be used only once. If the Flame Thrower is used, you may remove the rubble and go to **364**.

If you decide to do this, make a note that one Flame Thrower is now 'out of fuel'. You'd best be careful here since, as we have already told you, there's no guarantee that the rubble won't be back again if the Lemmings retrace their steps!

If you think the Lemmings would do better to retrace their steps and try another path, then go to **229**.

390
At last the Lemmings find themselves out in the open – and not a moment too soon! They all breathe a sigh of relief. Go to **387**.

391
The Skiers step up to the edge of the slope, and the other Lemmings grab hold of them. With a bit of luck, the Skiers will be able to guide them all down to the bottom. But hang on a moment, how many Skiers are there in the party?

If there are 5 or more, then go to **220**.

If there are less than 5, go to **321**.

392
Oh dear, oh dear ... more paths ... more shadows ... is there no end to it all? (Hee, hee!) Still, now your

choice is down to one of two: bear right (go to **363**) or bear left (go to **332**).

393

The Magno Boots Lemming steps up to the mast, which luckily is made of steel, and begins to walk up the side of it. Easy when you know how, isn't it?!

In no time at all, the Magno Boots is standing at the top. Go to **161**.

394

The spaceship hasn't been used in ages and is in a dreadful state of repair. The Lemmings will have to get to the bridge before the spaceship can take them down to the planet, but the way is blocked where a ceiling has collapsed.

Go to **359**.

395

Welcome to the Space Zone. This is the home of the Space Lemmings, those bold explorers of the Lemming Final Frontier. These Lemmings like nothing more than floating around, dodging the asteroids and exposing themselves to gamma-rays and all manner of dangerous things.

This is the start of the Space Zone. Before you go any further, you must select the Lemmings that will go on this part of the quest. How many you can have depends on the number of Lemmings you finished the last zone with. Simply trade in the Lemmings you already have for the new ones listed below on a one-for-one basis. If this is the first zone you have visited, then you may choose 50 Lemmings.

Lemmings available in the Space Zone

Attractor	Floater	Laser Blaster
Magno Boots	Mortar	Super Lem!
Jet Pack	Roper	Platformer

Once you have done this, make a note of the ones you have chosen, then go to **297**.

396

'Clang!!!' The Miner's pick hits iron. A large slab blocks the tunnel. There's no getting through this way. Worse than that, the Miner's pick has broken and may not be used again.

This Lemming is not removed from the party strength, but it may not be used again until we say so. If this leaves you with no Miners ... Oops!

Your adventure ends here

Of course, if you've got lots of them, you can go to **230** and have another go.

397

Scratchy bushes covered in vicious-looking thorns crowd in at the sides of the track.

What will the Lemmings do now? They can keep on following the path (go to **293**). Or they can try to retrace their steps (go to **248**).

398
Tonnes of rock thunder down the cliffside, engulfing both the Miner and the Basher (make sure you remove them from the party).

The other Lemmings look on in silence until the Herdman simply shouts: 'Back!'

Without a sound, the Lemmings turn around and walk back towards the forest path. Go to **310**.

399
In goes the Diver, and for a few moments all that the other Lemmings can see is a steady stream of bubbles coming to the surface of the small (but obviously very deep) pool.

Suddenly . . . go to **65**.

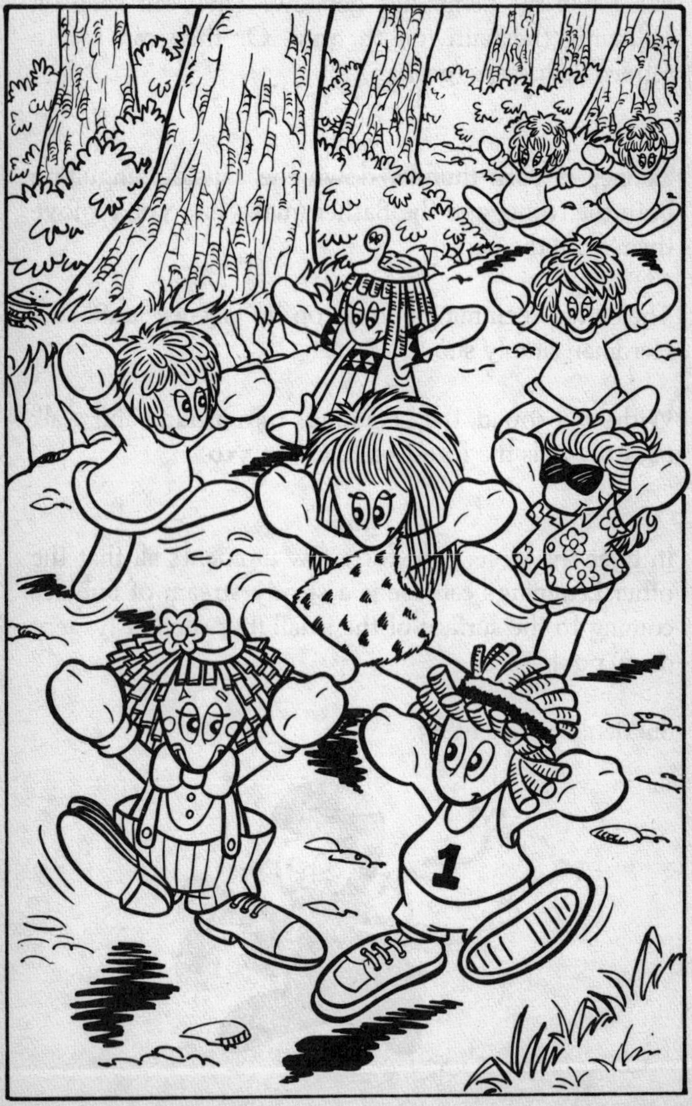
1

'Yippee!'

Some other Puffins

BEETHOVEN'S 2ND
Robert Tine

The Newton family are quite happy as dog people. But never in a million years did George Newton think they would be puppy people.

Enter Beethoven, followed by his friend, Missy, and their four St Bernard puppies. They are cuter than cute and messier than anything. None the less, just like Beethoven, George and his family quickly grow to love them all.

It's a big thing to look after so many dogs. It's an even bigger thing when there are nasty people around who want to put the puppies into breeding kennels, which means it's down to Beethoven and George to save the day!

STARGATE
Dean Devlin, Roland Emmerich and Sheila Black

The StarGate – its powerful secret riddle hidden for 10,000 years – has been uncovered. Brilliant archaeologist Daniel Jackson and fearless Colonel Jack O'Neil are the mismatched duo who lead a military team through the Gate to the unknown. Millions of light years from Earth, they discover a human society enslaved by the tyrannical ancient Egyptian god Ra. Locked into battle against his high-tech force the team must fight for their lives. Even if they survive, will they ever get home again?

SONIC THE HEDGEHOG ADVENTURE GAMEBOOK 3
SONIC V. ZONIK

Nigel Gross and Jon Sutherland

The Green Hill Zone is under attack from a new enemy. Reports come in of a fast-moving blue creature bashing everything in sight. Surely this can't be Sonic? Or has Robotnik cooked up another monstrous plan to crack the blue wonder?

It's up to you to find out. Use your speed, skill and agility in this part-story, part-game adventure. But think fast and move quickly — only the best can keep up with Sonic.

SONIC THE HEDGEHOG ADVENTURE GAMEBOOK 4
THE ZONE ZAPPER

Nigel Gross and Jon Sutherland

It's not unusual for Robotnik to go round messing up the Green Hill Zone. This time, however, he's built a brand-new machine which turns everything good into bad — even Tails! Sonic faces the fight of his life with his best friends. Will they survive and will he?

Think fast and act quickly — Sonic's going to need all the help he can get!